This is the story of Kareem Adbul-Jabbar.

Author Phil Pepe first met Abdul-Jabbar when he was Lew Alcindor, a 13-year-old who stood 6'8" tall. Pepe has been following Abdul-Jabbar's career ever since. Here's the complete story of the tall, soft-voiced young man who is a great basketball player—three times the NBA's Most Valuable Player in his first five years—an idealistic citizen deeply concerned with the role of blacks in American life and sports, and a man whose pride in his African heritage and devotion to his religious beliefs are unmistakable.

KAREEM ABDUL-JABBAR

BY PHIL PEPE

original title: STAND TALL

tempo
books

Madison School Library

GROSSET & DUNLAP, INC.
Publishers   New York

PUBLISHED SIMULTANEOUSLY IN CANADA

ORIGINALLY PUBLISHED BY GROSSET & DUNLAP, INC. AS

STAND TALL—THE LEW ALCINDOR STORY

LIBRARY OF CONGRESS CATALOG CARD NUMBER: 71-120422

ISBN: 0-448-05351-9

TEMPO BOOKS IS REGISTERED IN THE U.S. PATENT OFFICE

PRINTED IN THE UNITED STATES OF AMERICA

To all the kids for whom the great American game of basketball has provided a way out of the ghetto.

CONTENTS

INTRODUCTION

It is the first blush of spring, 1961, a warm, sunny, lazy afternoon, and I am sitting at my desk in the sports department of the New York *World Telegram & Sun* and my mind is cluttered with all the thoughts usually associated with young men in the spring.

Somewhere off in the distance a telephone is ringing, interrupting my reverie, and now I am on the telephone and the muffled voice on the other end of the receiver is saying he is with the New York City Catholic Youth Organization and am I planning to cover the game at Fordham University Saturday in which college basketball players from the New York-New Jersey area will play against players from Pennsylvania, and I say of course I am, and he asks if I know there is a game for the best high school players in New York City, and I say I do.

"You might be interested in the third game we have scheduled," the CYO man is saying. "It's for grammar schools, one team representing Brooklyn and Queens and one for Manhattan and the Bronx. We've got one kid on the Brooklyn-Queens team who is 14 years old and is six feet, seven inches, and one kid on the Manhattan-Bronx team who is 13 and 6-8."

"How soon can you have the two boys in my office for a story and pictures?" I ask.

An hour and a half later, I was setting eyes on Lew Alcindor for the first time. In the sports pages of the *World Telegram & Sun* of Tuesday, April 4, 1961, appeared the first story ever written about the young man who was destined to change the face of basketball.

The story, as it appeared then, follows:

"Lewis Alcindor is a typically average 13-year-old who stands six feet, eight inches tall.

"He 'towers' over Pat Heelan, who turned 14

last week, but alas, measures only 6-7 on the kitchen wall.

"Both are basketball players. Surprise!

"There are college coaches who would take both boys right now—if they could. But the boys are in grammar school and it will be a four-year wait while the Tall Ones make life miserable for opposing coaches in high school—Lewis in Power Memorial, Pat in St. Francis Prep.

"These choices, incidentally, are definite, final and irrevocable. Rival coaches please note.

"Lewis and Pat have met on a basketball court once—Alcindor for St. Jude's in Manhattan, Heelan for Our Lady of Angels in Brooklyn —in a CYO tournament.

"'They beat us by four points,' Lewis sadly reports.

"'That's right,' beamed Pat, looking down at the questioner from his lofty perch. 'We both scored about 17,' Heelan added as Lewis nodded.

"They'll meet again Saturday in the Fordham gym in a battle of young skyscrapers that alone is worth the price of admission. It's the first game of a CYO-sponsored tripleheader called the Metropolitan Basketball Festival.

"Heelan plays for the Brooklyn diocese

against Alcindor's team of grammar school all-stars from the Manhattan diocese. After that game is a high school all-star game, followed by a college all-star game with such as St. John's Tony Jackson, Providence's Johnny Egan, Holy Cross' George Blaney and Tim Shea, and St. Joseph's Jack Egan and Vince Kempton.

"Still, it shouldn't be a surprise if the young giants steal the show from the older fellows. And don't get the idea that Lewis and Pat are just a couple of big kids.

"Heelan led OLA to a 30-0 record, including championships in the St. Francis and LaSalle grammar school tournaments. Pat once scored 51 points in a game.

"Lewis had a high of 34 in leading St. Jude's to a 13-4 record. But basketball isn't everything.

" 'I want to get an engineering degree,' says Lewis, who had a 94 average on his mid-year report card, a disturbing dip from 96.6 last semester. 'Yes, I've thought about pro ball. Everybody does. But I know I can't play basketball forever.'

"Pat, a B student, is undecided about his future, but says, 'I've thought seriously about the brotherhood.'

"Both boys admit they were involved in the usual number of boyish scraps while they were growing up . . . and up . . . and . . .

" 'I had a few fights,' Alcindor says timidly. 'The kids used to tease me about being so big. They don't anymore.'

"As the parent of any growing teenager can readily appreciate, keeping the boys clothed and fed is a full-time job.

" 'Lewis is always hungry,' says his mom, who's almost six feet tall. Pop stands 6-2½. 'He doesn't eat much, but often. We have to get his clothes at a special place and his shoes (size 16) come from Brockton, Mass.'

" 'Pat wears a size 32 suit, extra long, and a size 13 shoe,' says his strapping 6-4 dad, a giant in his day.

"Both boys are aware they may grow to seven feet, but neither is concerned.

" 'I'm satisfied with whatever I am,' says Pat. 'I wouldn't mind being seven feet tall.'

"Neither would Lewis, he says, although he has already become aware of the problems of being so tall.

" 'I've outgrown my bed,' he says."

In the years that followed, a great change came over Lew Alcindor, not the least of which was a great personal conversion, adopting a new religion and changing to the Islamic name of Kareem Abdul-Jabbar.

I watched all of these changes come about, mostly from the distance that separated us in miles and in years and in ideas. We had both come a long way from the days when he was Lew Alcindor.

I watched him grow to 7 feet, 2 inches tall; I watched him become a nationally known high school star, then lead UCLA to three consecutive national collegiate championships; I watched him sign a $1,250,000 contract with the Milwaukee Bucks of the National Basketball Association. And while I watched, I thought about that first meeting often, and that first story. I had followed his progress closely, with curiosity and interest, the curiosity of a newspaperman, the interest of—I thought, I hoped —a friend.

I watched him play several times for Power Memorial High School.

I was there the day he ended all the wild speculation and announced he had decided to matriculate at UCLA.

During the summer before he left for California, I took him to Shea Stadium to meet members of the New York Mets and Los Angeles Dodgers.

I saw him play as a freshman at UCLA.

I interviewed him at great length for a magazine story following that first unsettling, disturbing year away from home, a year filled with frustration and unrest.

I visited with him in Philadelphia at the all-star game in his rookie season as a pro.

The years flew by all too quickly and the change from Lew Alcindor to Kareem Abdul-Jabbar was great. He grew in many dimensions, not only physical, although that, too. I have watched him develop as a basketball player and as a person. I have watched him mature from a boy to a man, an intelligent, aware, sensitive, concerned man.

Often he was troubled, often he was hostile. His critics are legion, but too quickly they forget that he is young, famous, seven feet tall and black. The world isn't exactly overflowing with people who know what it's like to be young, famous, seven feet tall and black.

Today, he is a mature man, a sensitive man, a controversial man. He is, at once, the most dominant figure in professional basketball and one of the most recognized people in the world.

In the summer of 1971, he gave up his chance

to relax. Instead, he went on an exhibition tour of six African countries, at the request of the State Department. He feels great pride in his African ancestry and heritage.

His decision to embrace the Islamic faith was not done quickly, thoughtlessly or by whim. And his new name, Kareem Abdul-Jabbar, was carefully chosen. Kareem means "generous," Abdul means "strong," and Jabbar means "servant of Allah." The choice says much about the man himself, and about the ideals he cherishes.

His performance on the court speaks for itself. In his first five years as a professional, he won three Most Valuable Player awards and two scoring championships while averaging 30.5 points per game, the highest lifetime scoring average of any player in NBA history. He also has averaged more points per game in the playoffs (29.7) than anybody else. And it seemed that his best years were still ahead of him.

It was during the 1971-72 season, after Abdul-Jabbar had led the Milwaukee Bucks to their first championship, that his coach, Larry Costello, said of Kareem: "He is the greatest basketball player ever."

This, then, is the story of Kareem Abdul-

Jabbar, who may well be the greatest basketball player ever.

1
DECISION DAY

It was not yet eight o'clock in the morning, but the hot sun was shining brightly, splashing the city's streets with its brilliance. It was going to be a hot one, this Tuesday, May 4, 1965.

Already, the tall young man could feel the trickle of perspiration under his arms as he walked along Dyckman Street in upper Manhattan, heading for the subway. Then he would begin the familiar, 20-minute ride that would take him downtown to Power Memorial High School.

Today, as every other day, there would be

the usual stares and he would try, as he always did, to ignore them. He would open a book and read, trying to shut out everything around him. Today, it would not be easy.

Perhaps it was more than the hot sun that was causing his discomfort this morning. Perhaps it was the anxiety, the uneasiness he felt about what lay before him.

At noon, he was scheduled to be in the Power Memorial gymnasium to meet with the press. Coach Jack Donohue had made the arrangements, had called the newspapers to tell them that the press conference had been arranged, a press conference for a 17-year-old. It seemed ludicrous, even to the 17-year-old, but coach Donohue had convinced him this was the proper way, the only way to handle it, to put a halt to all the speculation of the last few weeks ... months ... years; to put an end to all the silly, annoying questions.

As he headed for the subway, feeling damp and uncomfortable and a little confused and frightened, Lew Alcindor was conscious of a voice behind him.

"Hey, Lewie," said the voice and when he turned, Lew Alcindor could see a man standing in the doorway of a tavern. "Where ya gonna go ta college?"

4

For the past six months it had been like this, people asking him that question hundreds of times. He was stopped on the street, called at from passing cabs and mail trucks, approached in the subway. Always the answer was the same. He did not know which college, of the hundreds who wanted his services, he would attend.

Today he did know. He would reveal his choice in less than five hours and the speculation—and the endless questions—would be over. He knew, but when the man asked him, he shrugged his shoulders and spread his huge hands in a gesture that proclaimed, without words, that he had not yet made his decision.

At the age of 17, Lew Alcindor was a celebrity in his home town. It is the largest, busiest city in the world, yet people always seemed to have time to stop and stare at this awesome, easily recognized figure, to ask those endless inane questions.

"How tall are you?"

"Hey, how's the weather up there?"

It was cruel. It was rude. But Lew Alcindor had learned to accept the questions . . . not to like them, but to accept them. He enjoyed being recognized—anyone would—but he did not enjoy being badgered, interrupted, mocked, abused, stared at and made the butt of silly jokes like he was some kind of curiosity or sideshow freak. He longed for privacy. He longed to be allowed to grow up like any other teenager.

It was, he was learning, the price of being a seven-footer in a five-feet, 10-inch world. Somebody once said he was no different than any other 17-year-old high school senior who happened to stand seven feet, one inch tall. And it was as if his unusual height gave people a license for cruelty and rudeness.

Everything had happened too quickly for Lew Alcindor; too quickly for a 17-year-old to learn to cope with all the attention he was receiving at such a young age. He could not go to a movie without people gawking at him. He could not sit and drink a soda without people asking him some silly question. He could not go to a basketball game at Madison Square Garden without being surrounded by reporters, photographers or the leeches who try to curry favor with high school basketball players in the hope of being able to deliver them to some college ... for a price. He could not even walk down the street without hearing, for the thousandth time, some inane remark.

There was no place Lew Alcindor could hide,

nowhere to turn for help, no one who had experienced these problems. Yes, there was one, but Wilt Chamberlain was too remote in years and distance and importance. Lew Alcindor would have to face it alone.

Once it was fun being so tall. He was 13 and a student at St. Jude's grammar school in upper Manhattan and he stood six feet, eight inches tall, and it brought him attention and recognition at an age when a boy hurts for attention and recognition. It gave him a strange feeling of pride and power when people looked up at him in wonderment, and when they made jokes about his height, in his innocence, he laughed along with them.

Soon it was no longer fun. It stopped being fun when he was a sophomore at Power Memorial High School.

It wasn't only the comments and jokes that were beginning to annoy him. Now there were other things. Requests for interviews and pictures, letters and telephone calls from college coaches, scouts and hangers-on and the constant speculation and wild rumors in the newspapers; rumors of deals made and of imaginary, surreptitious meetings with alumni and representatives of colleges all over the country; rumors of presents received and

7

promises made by colleges when college was the farthest thing from his mind. He was grateful, then, for Mr. Donohue.

Young Jack Donohue was Alcindor's coach at Power Memorial High School. He was wise enough to anticipate the problems that would confront Alcindor in the years ahead, thoughtful enough to attempt to overcome these problems and stubborn enough to stick to his unique and much-criticized plan.

He had set up a protective wall around the boy, refusing to allow him to speak to the press, college coaches, scouts, even the man on the street. He screened all scholarship offers and anyone who managed to penetrate that protective wall and reach either Lewis or his parents, was told politely, but firmly, to speak to Mr. Donohue.

More than one stranger was ejected, sometimes forcibly, when discovered loitering around Power Memorial's gym. And even friends and acquaintances of Donohue, extended the privilege of being permitted to watch Power work out, were banished, their privilege revoked, if caught so much as trying to pass the time of day with Alcindor. A rule, Jack Donohue decreed, is a rule and it was to be adhered to without exception.

For his handling of the most celebrated high school basketball player of his time, Donohue was severely criticized by some, fervently applauded by others.

Right or wrong, Jack Donohue had established the pattern that would guide Lew Alcindor's life for the next eight years. Whether it was good for Lew or bad for him is open to dispute . . . and has been disputed on numerous occasions. But one thing is indisputable.

Lew Alcindor was thrust into a situation, not of his own making, that transformed him from childhood to manhood long before his time. If he seemed, at times, unequipped to handle the transformation, it must be remembered that he was still only 15. Few other 15-year-olds would have been able to handle it. No other 15-year-old ever had to try.

2
YOUTH

Perhaps a pediatrician could have looked at Lew Alcindor the day he came into the world and predicted he would grow to be more than seven feet tall.

Perhaps a fortune teller could have looked at Lew Alcindor the day he came into the world and said: "Here is a child who will become one of the greatest, most dominant athletes in the history of sports."

The day Lew Alcindor came into the world was April 16, 1947, and from that first day, the thing that immediately attracted attention was his size. He weighed 12 pounds, 11 ounces, and was 22½ inches long. On his birth certificate, he was listed as Ferdinand Lewis Alcindor, Jr., but from that first day to this, to his parents he was Lewis.

Without the practiced eye of a pediatrician or the foresight of a fortune teller, there was little else that could have been interpreted as any kind of omen. His father, Ferdinand Lewis Alcindor, Sr., was a strapping six feet, two and one-half inches in height, taller than the average man, but hardly a giant. His mother, Cora Douglas Alcindor, was a handsome woman, strikingly tall at 5-11.

It was from his father's father that Lewis inherited his great height. Lew never knew his grandfather, but he heard his father talk of him often. Grandfather Alcindor was a regal-looking man, six feet, eight inches tall, and the proud possessor of a full, flowing mustache.

Lew's grandfather came from Trinidad. The name Alcindor is Moorish. It means "firebird," a bird that rises from its own ashes.

The year Lewis Alcindor was born the Dodgers were still in Brooklyn, World War II had just ended, Korea, Viet Nam and Laos were the strange names of faraway lands on a map in a geography book, and the National

11

Basketball Association still had not been formed.

There were, in 1947, two professional basketball leagues in direct competition for talent and attendance. The Basketball Association of America, formed in June of 1946, had completed its first season of play with the Philadelphia Warriors, of the Eastern Division, defeating the Chicago Stags, of the Western Division, four games to one for the championship.

The big scorer of the BAA was Philadelphia's Joe Fulks, a 6-5 jump shooter who averaged 23.2 points a game. And there were only 17 players in the league who stood 6-7 or taller.

The rival league was the National Basketball League, which had been in existence since 1937. The Chicago American Gears won the NBL title in 1947, led by the game's first effective big man, 6-10 George Mikan, who averaged 16.5 points a game as a rookie.

Three seasons later, the two leagues merged to form the National Basketball Association. When Minneapolis defeated Syracuse, four games to two, for the championship that concluded the first year of play in the NBA, Ferdinand Lewis Alcindor, Jr., a young man destined to play a significant role in the history of the league, was just three years old.

For the first three and a half years of his life, Lewis Alcindor lived on 111th Street and Seventh Avenue in New York's Harlem. He has no recollections of those three and a half years, naturally, and no neighbor has come forth to say he recalls Lew Alcindor, age three, dribbling a basketball down Broadway. Nor did a pediatrician or fortune teller come forth to make any bold predictions. It was impossible to look at one so young and discover the intense competitive drive and the fierce desire that was beginning, even then, to grow within him.

When Lew was three and a half his father moved the family to the Dyckman Housing Project, a development in the Inwood section of Upper Manhattan that comprised seven 14-story buildings with 12 apartments on a floor. Life in the Dyckman project was pleasant and uncomplicated. There were hundreds of youngsters living in the project and there was never a dearth of playmates or playgrounds.

Situated near the Harlem River Drive, the Dyckman project was just a few blocks from 193rd Street and Fort Tryon Park. And a short distance away was the Cloisters, the museum of medieval art.

As an only child whose parents both worked, Lew never wanted for anything. His childhood was one of contentment. The Inwood section was a mixture of second and third generation Irish and Italians with a scattering of blacks— "The ghetto had not reached there yet," Alcindor said recently—a proportion of six whites to every black. Racial injustice and bigotry, which would eventually, and inevitably, touch him as it touches all blacks, had not yet surfaced.

His closest friends were white, but Lew thought of them not as whites, but as kids in the project. And they regarded him in the same manner. In this carefree existence, he was never aware that he was different because of the color of his skin; he was aware that he was different only because of his height. He towered over the kids his own age and most of the kids two and three years older.

When it was time to go to school, his parents enrolled Lewis in St. Jude's, a Catholic grammar school run by the Presentation Sisters. The story they tell is that in his first day at St. Jude's, a teacher spotted Lewis in the back of the room.

"You, there," she said, "please sit down."

And Lewis is said to have replied for posterity, "But I am sitting down."

It wasn't until he was in the third grade that Lew came face-to-face with race prejudice. The

14

signs, at first, were subtle, almost innocent. Every two or three weeks he and his father would climb aboard the No. 100 bus and ride 70 blocks down Broadway to get their hair cut in a Harlem barbershop.

Lewis was only eight, but even a boy of eight can figure out that there must be an easier way. One day, in his youthful ignorance, the son said to the father: "Why can't we go to one of the barbers in the neighborhood? Why do we have to go all the way to 125th Street?"

And the father, who knew, just as all black fathers know, that the question would come some day, and who had prepared for that day, was ready with his answer.

"Lewis," he said, "number one is that the white barbers in the neighborhood might not cut our hair the way we want it, and number two is that they might not want to cut it at all."

That was all, quickly, simply and painlessly. The question had come and the answer had been given and somehow the young and innocent boy was not so young or innocent anymore.

Later, when he was older and more aware and less innocent, Lewis Alcindor thought back and remembered that and other things. He remembered the day, when he was five, that he and his mother went to see his father graduate from Juilliard, the most famous, most honored music school in the country. Lewis remembered how proud he was of his father that day and he remembers how proud his mother was and mostly he remembers how happy his father had seemed.

His father played the baritone horn and trombone, he had sung with the Hall Johnson Chorus, had performed with the Senior Musicians Symphony at Carnegie Hall and he had studied piano and conducting at Juilliard. It never occurred to Lewis, at the time, that working first as a bill collector for a furniture company and later as police sergeant for the Transit Authority, his father was wasting his exceptional talents, that he was not working at what he loved best. Nor did it occur to Lewis why his father was not doing the thing for which he worked so hard and had studied so many hours.

Later, when he was older and more aware and did understand, it pained Lewis to think of his father not working in the field he loved, the field for which he was trained. "It makes me sad," he said, "to realize that my father never got to do what he wanted to do in life."

But haircuts in Harlem and his father's resignation to a lesser lot in life were but subtle, indirect, impersonal signs. The direct sign would come when Lew was in the seventh grade at St. Jude's. And it would brush him casually . . . like a building falling on his chest.

Lew Alcindor had a friend at St. Jude's, a white kid, and in the way kids do, they took an oath to be best friends. Not a blood oath, not even an oral oath, but a kid's oath. They sought each other out and were inseparable playmates and classmates. It was a beautiful thing in the way that only kid things can be beautiful.

But kids grow up . . . sooner or later, they grow up. It happened to Lew Alcindor and his friend in the seventh grade.

"I started being friendly with two black kids and he became pretty tight with a clique of whites," Lew remembers. "That was OK; kids are always coming together and drifting apart through school; no big deal. I didn't attach any racial overtones to it."

But there were racial overtones, as Lew was to discover harshly. One day a group of boys, including Lew and his white friend, were in the school's lunchroom, horsing around. Typical kid stuff. Lew was pushing and getting pushed, all

in fun, and accidentally one of the boys Lew
pushed rammed into his white friend.

"He got up, walked over and slapped me in
the face," Lew recalls. "So, I slapped him back
and I figured that was the end of that. I was
wrong."

Later that afternoon, Alcindor was walking
home and he heard a voice behind him.

"Nigger."

When Lewis turned around, there was his
"best friend" with several other white boys.

"Nigger."

They shouted louder now.

"Blackie. Black boy. Nigger."

All the way home, Alcindor heard the
taunts, the insults, the words that all blacks
hear in time. Lew was crushed, his youthful
innocence shattered. He had grown up.

By then, basketball had become very much a
part of Lew Alcindor's life. His year, as it
would for the next 20 years or so, revolved
around the basketball season. His day revolved
around basketball practice. Everything else was
secondary to basketball.

Basketball discovered Lewis Alcindor quite
by accident when he was in the fourth grade.
But it was an accident that had to happen.
Before the fourth grade, he had been active in

other sports—swimming, skating, playing Little League baseball. His dad had been a good athlete—a swimmer, a handball player and a track man. Basketball had never been a part of the elder Alcindor's life and about the only basketball Lew learned from his father was how to dribble.

Then came the fourth grade. Because his parents both worked and there was no one to care for Lewis, he was sent to Holy Providence School in Cornwell Heights, Pa. The student body at Holy Providence was made up, ostensibly, of black ghetto kids from Philadelphia, Baltimore and Washington, D.C.

Standing five feet, four inches tall at age nine, Lewis Alcindor was the second tallest boy in the eight-grade school. It made him a desired teammate when the boys got together for a game of basketball.

At Holy Providence, Lew learned the game from scratch and he learned it from ghetto kids. He learned to play basketball the way it was played in ghetto schoolyards. He learned to pull, push and tug. He learned to use his elbow and his hips. It was an education.

Back in St. Jude's for the fifth grade, Lew was ready to apply what he had learned at Holy Providence for the benefit of the St.

19

Jude's grammar school team. Only one player, an eighth grader, was taller than Lew, so he was invited to try out for the team. It was here that he came under the influence of a kind, patient, hard-working man named Farrell Hopkins.

Farrell Hopkins recognized in Lewis Alcindor a rare opportunity for a coach. Lewis Alcindor was the dream all coaches dream, a player willing to work hard and sacrifice for success. At his height, and with four more years to grow and improve before he graduated from St. Jude's, Lew was a player a coach could work with and develop. Alcindor could guarantee St. Jude's success in New York City's Catholic Youth Organization grammar school basketball program. And so Farrell Hopkins began working with Alcindor, but he did it as much for Lew Alcindor as for St. Jude's and Farrell Hopkins.

At first Lew was awkward, as awkward as any kid who is growing too fast to become accustomed to his new body. And Farrell Hopkins put him on a rigid program of weight-lifting for strength, tennis and rope-skipping for speed, coordination and reflexes.

Basketball practice would begin when school let out at three and it would end at five. But

Alcindor, his desire to improve growing as rapidly as his body, often stayed until six and seven o'clock to practice alone in the gym. In the sixth grade he had grown to six feet and he had become Farrell Hopkins' pet project.

One day after Lew had missed an easy layup, coach Hopkins took him aside. "Look, Lewis," he said paternally. "Making layups is just a matter of practice. If you miss a layup at your height you look ridiculous. You only give people something to laugh at."

Farrell Hopkins had touched Lewis Alcindor's sensitive nerve. He didn't want to be laughed at. He practiced layups by the hour, shooting them by the hundreds, until he had perfected the shot with his left hand as well as his right.

In New York City, the Catholic high schools which offer scholarships recruit basketball players with as much fervor as some colleges. High School coaches blanket the area, scouting grammar school teams for talent. By the time he had completed the seventh grade, Alcindor stood an imposing 6-6. The fact that he had made St. Jude's honor roll every year since the fifth grade was another plus in his favor. Every high school basketball coach in the city who was able to offer a scholarship knew about him ... and wanted him.

He was wanted at Archbishop Molloy and Power Memorial, the two schools with the most powerful teams in New York City. The Hill School, an exclusive and prestigious private prep in Pottstown, Pa., wanted Lew to become the first black athlete in its history.

Other schools made their pitch but in the end it narrowed down to Molloy and Power. When Lew was a senior at St. Jude's, his friend Art Kenney, who lived in the Dyckman project and was a freshman at Power Memorial, took Lew to meet Power's coach, Jack Donohue.

Alcindor liked Donohue immediately. He was a young, jolly-faced Irishman and a fine, intense coach who had a reputation for turning out winning teams at Power. Another factor was travel. Archbishop Molloy was in Jamaica, Queens. To get there, Lewis would have to take two buses and the subway, a trip that would take an hour and a half. Power, on the other hand, was a short, direct, 20-minute subway ride from home. To Jack Donohue's delight Lewis said he would enroll at Power the following September.

When September rolled around, Donohue

was even more delighted. Over the summer, Lewis Alcindor had grown a few more inches. He now stood six feet, 10 inches tall.

3

JACK DONOHUE

Jack Donohue is a man of many prejudices. He is prejudiced against laziness. He is bigoted against a lack of hustle. He abhors indifference. He detests complacency. He is intolerant of people who take the easy way. He is biased against defeatism.

Those are Jack Donohue's prejudices; his only prejudices. He does not care if you are black, white, brown, red, purple or polka dot as long as you try. He does not care if you are tall, short, fat, skinny, blond or black-haired as long as you work hard. He does not care if your parents were born in this country or not, if you go to a church, a synagogue or a mosque, if you speak with an accent, a brogue, a drawl or a lisp as long as you try to win; as long as you don't try to cheat him, use him or put one over on him.

Jack Donohue is now, and always has been, his own man; a man obsessed with winning; a man who always did what he thought was right and never concerned himself with the consequences. He created controversy. He took a stand and refused to back down. You could agree with him or disagree with him, you could accuse him of being narrow, misinformed and illogical, but you could never doubt that Jack Donohue was doing what he sincerely believed was best for his players.

— Lew Alcindor gave Jack Donohue a lot of pleasure. He also caused him a lot of grief. There are many who believe that Donohue would have been better off if he had never met Lew Alcindor. Jack Donohue is not one of them.

For several years before Alcindor came along, Donohue had been turning out winning basketball teams at Power Memorial High School, a Catholic school in midtown Manhattan run by the Irish Christian Brothers. Young, ambitious and hard-working, Donohue was quickly gaining a reputation among coaches. His teams were always well-coached, always competitive. He had won the championship of the New York City Catholic high school league—the CHSSA—before he had ever heard of Alcindor. He had sent dozens of players on to college. But he had not yet gained a national reputation. That was about to change.

Donohue had been hearing about a tall player at St. Jude's grammar school. He had also been hearing about a tall kid who had been playing in the Power Memorial gym on Sundays with Arthur Kenney, a 6-8 Power freshman. It turned out that the young man at St. Jude's and the young man playing at Power on Sundays was one and the same.

"His name is Alcindor," Kenney told Donohue. "He lives in my building. He's a senior at St. Jude's and he's interested in coming to Power. I'll bring him around some day."

A few days later, Jack Donohue was setting eyes on Lew Alcindor for the first time and he knew, instinctively, that someday the boy would be a great basketball player. Actually, it didn't take much instinct at all. All that was required was fairly good eyesight. Alcindor stood six feet, eight inches tall and he was only 13 years old.

Largely because of his friend, Art Kenney, Alcindor decided to attend Power Memorial and for the next four years, Jack Donohue would be the central figure in the life of Lewis Alcindor just as Lewis Alcindor would be the central figure in the life of Jack Donohue.

"I had only seen him play once in grammar school," Donohue recalls, "and he wasn't very good. But he was big and he was interested in becoming a basketball player. He got a great start in grammar school. His coach, Farrell Hopkins, did a great job with him. Lewis was not babied along, which would have been easy to do with a kid that big and the star of the team and all."

There were two things about Alcindor that impressed Donohue immediately. "He could run and he could catch the ball, which is very important for a big man. His father had helped. Lewis played a lot of handball and did a lot of swimming and we got him jumping rope to improve his coordination. The one thing he always had was this tremendous pride, which was the big difference between him and a lot of other kids. He didn't mind hard work and long hours of practice."

Alcindor did not develop overnight at Power. For weeks, Donohue could not make up his mind whether to play him on the varsity or junior varsity in his freshman year. Unable to solve the dilemma, Donohue consulted Danny Buckley, a veteran high school coach and a rival of Donohue's at LaSalle Academy in lower Manhattan.

"Danny, you've had big kids," Donohue said. "Do you think I should play my big kid on the varsity?"

"Will you make the playoffs without him?" Buckley asked.

"No," said Donohue.

"Will you make the playoffs with him?"

"No."

"Then don't play him," Buckley advised. "This is a tough league. He could get hurt."

Donohue considered Buckley's advice, but still had not made up his mind as he prepared to meet LaSalle in the season opener. Right up to game time, he still had not made up his mind. He had Alcindor bring both his varsity and jayvee uniforms to the game. Finally, Donohue made his decision. Alcindor would start at center for Power.

It was not an auspicious debut for the young man who was destined to make his mark in basketball in high school, college and as a pro. Power lost the game and Alcindor was completely outplayed by the LaSalle center, a 6-9 kid named Val Reid, who went on to play at Syracuse University. But Donohue did not regret his decision.

"You don't have to worry about that kid," Danny Buckley told Donohue after the game. "He can take it. He's going to be all right."

And Alcindor was all right. He helped Power make the playoffs, averaging 11 points a game as a freshman.

"He was less than an average varsity player," Donohue remembers. "But there was nobody to compare him with. After all, he was only 14. But he was 6-10 and he was more of a psychological threat than anything else. The other teams didn't realize he wasn't too good, but he was there and so big and they had to be concerned with him."

In his sophomore year, Alcindor started attracting attention. The improvement from his freshman year to his sophomore year, says Donohue, was unbelievable. "Most big boys are awkward," Donohue says, "But after his freshman year, you couldn't say that about Lewie anymore. Sure, he had given talent. But others have had it and never developed it. He did because his biggest asset was tremendous

29

pride. I knew in his sophomore year that Lewie was going to be something special."

Alcindor's sophomore year was also the start of a three-year controversy that would attract nation-wide attention and would split people into two factions—those who supported Donohue and those who opposed him.

Alcindor's sophomore year would also be his last as a trouble-free youth, his last before a slowly-widening breach began developing between player and coach and would erupt with national attention some eight years later.

There is this that must be understood about Jack Donohue. He stood rigidly behind a theory that no man was more important than the team. And he never deviated from that theory in practice. The most important members of the team were not the starters, they were not the tallest players, they were not the highest scorers. They were the seniors, the boys who had worked harder for a longer period of time.

Toward this end, Donohue had a simple, but effective, initiation for sophomores. They were responsible for carrying balls to and from practice and it was a ludicrous sight to see Lew Alcindor, seven feet tall by then, lugging a bagful of basketballs to and from practice.

When there were tickets to basketball games

at Madison Square Garden, they were distributed first to seniors, then to juniors and then, if there were any remaining, to sophomores.

After practice or a game, Donohue would drive some players home. Again, it was seniors first and Donohue might give Art Kenney a ride while Alcindor, who lived in the same building as Kenney, would go by subway until he had served his initiation and earned the privilege of a ride home in his junior and senior years.

"I wasn't going to pick him up just because he was Lew Alcindor," Donohue explained. "He had to earn it by being around long enough."

If it seems like a cruel and contrived attempt to place himself ahead of the player, Donohue took pride in a remark Alcindor made after he had graduated from Power. "The one thing I'll always remember," Lew said, "is that I wasn't treated any differently than anybody else on the team."

A strict disciplinarian and a demanding coach, Donohue's voice could often be heard throughout the Power gym, above the noise of practice, reprimanding his tall and talented star.

"Off the court, off the court," he would bellow. "If you can't get back on defense, then get off the court."

During his sophomore year, Alcindor began to create his own excitement. The word travels fast on the basketball grapevine, and all over the country, particularly when coaches gathered, they were talking about the 15-year-old, seven-foot sophomore in New York. Power went through an unbeaten season and with each victory, interest in Alcindor grew commensurately. College coaches and scouts, newspapermen and photographers flocked to Power, hoping Lew would grant them an interview, a quick picture, even an acknowledging nod.

It was then that Donohue invoked his famous "no talk" ban. Nobody was permitted to talk to Alcindor without the coach's permission. And that meant nobody. Even friends of Donohue were ruled out of the gym if they so much as attempted to say, "Hi, Lew."

Even then, it was easier to get to the Shah of Iran than it was to get to Alcindor. By Donohue's decree, Alcindor granted no newspaper interviews. All letters sent to his home were forwarded, unopened, to coach Jack Donohue, in care of Power Memorial High School. College coaches and scouts who somehow managed to get Alcindor's home telephone number were told to talk to Mr. Donohue.

"It wasn't something that started with Lewie," Donohue insists. "I always had that rule. I had it when we had Waverly Davis (a 6-9 player who went on to Seattle University), but nobody realized it until Lewie came along. It wasn't so much for newspapers as it was for colleges. Without being imposed upon, he got as much publicity as he was going to get. I couldn't let him be subjected to all the scouts that wanted to talk to him. He was going to be out every night if I'd let him. My job was to filter things for him and I don't think it hurt him. He went to the school he wanted to go to anyway. And I did everything I could to get him to the school he wanted to go to and to see that he had some privacy. I did the same for every kid who ever played for me. They work hard for four seasons. They deserve anything I can do for them."

Donohue took his stand and the people who were affected—and many who weren't—took sides.

"You can't keep a kid in his shell," said Donohue's critics. "Talking to the press is a part of his education. What will he do when Donohue isn't around to protect him? He won't know how to talk to people."

"Donohue's doing the right thing," said his supporters. "Alcindor's just a kid. At his age, how can he be expected to separate the phonies from the legitimate people?"

One of Donohue's staunchest supporters was Joe Lapchick, the Original Celtic and, at the time, coach of St. John's University.

"It's great," Lapchick said. "Anywhere a basketball is bounced in this country, they know about this kid and it can get tough on a boy. He's lucky to have a strong-willed man like Jack steering his ship. It took Chamberlain five years before he realized how great it is to be with a winner. This kid is a winner and his head isn't out to here."

/ In later years, when he was asked about Donohue's ban on talking, Alcindor said he didn't mind it. "Things turned out all right," he said.

Lew's mother was grateful for Donohue's interference. "We know what getting a lot of publicity has done to other boys," she commented. "He think Mr. Donohue is a very capable man. We are with him 100 percent. When any of those cuckoos call, we tell them they'll have to speak to Mr. Donohue."

And what about Alcindor's relationship with

the press? "Sometimes I appreciated the reporters and other times I didn't. I got annoyed at them because of all the speculation about the college I would attend. They kept shooting ideas all over the place like a machine gun. I gave them credit for more sense than that. Then there were things that I appreciated. Like the publicity. I'm like everybody else, I like attention."

With the benefit of hindsight and free of coaching in high school, Donohue says "I'd do the same thing all over again if I was in that position. If I had let him talk to everyone, he would have lost his perspective. If I had let him free, he never would have had the chance to live like a normal 16-year-old or 17-year-old. Wasn't he entitled to that?"

While Donohue protected his star player and found himself in a position for which there was no precedent, player and coach seemed to be drawn together in a unity of thought, effort and end. They wanted to win ball games, as many as they could. Donohue, meanwhile, was determined to keep Alcindor from being swallowed up by the flesh peddlers who try to buy and sell basketball prospects like so many head of cattle. The coach worked hard to keep the player from becoming too impressed with himself, to realize that individual glory and achievements must be subordinated to team effort.

And the player seemed grateful to Donohue for the protection, for getting him to understand the importance of winning and for instilling in him an attitude of unselfishness which was to follow him throughout his basketball career. Each summer, Donohue would go to Friendship Farm, a basketball camp he ran in upstate New York. And for three straight summers, after his sophomore year, Alcindor went with him. For two summers he worked around the camp while he practiced three and four hours a day to improve his game. During the third summer, he worked as a counselor.

Even as a teenager, Lew Alcindor was a concerned young man, concerned with the plight of the black man in America, aware of the problems around him. And Jack Donohue never lost sight of Alcindor's concern and respected his star center for that concern.

Once, during a scrimmage, Alcindor and his pal, Art Kenney, got into a mild scuffle in which some half-hearted swings were exchanged. Donohue called an immediate halt to the practice.

"Gentlemen." he said, "I want no racial violence in the gym."

"Mr. Donohue?" said Lew. "How about peaceful demonstration, like CORE?"

"That's all right."

"Can I carry a placard?"

"OK," said Donohue, "but no big words."

Another time, the Power team was assembled to pose for a picture and Lew, for obvious reasons, was asked to step to the back.

"Mr. Donohue, are you prejudiced?"

"No," said the coach, "it's just that you're so damn tall."

On the outside, Donohue and Alcindor seemed to have a wonderful coach-player relationship. That was on the outside. On the inside, things were happening to Alcindor, things that would not come to light until he wrote his life story for *Sports Illustrated* after he had signed a professional contract, four years after he had left Donohue and Power Memorial behind him.

In his story, Alcindor said he resented being forced to go to Friendship Farm and that Donohue had called him a name, *that* name. It happened, Alcindor said, during halftime of Power's game with DeMatha High in Hyattsville, Md.

"We played rotten," Alcindor wrote, "and I played rottener than anybody, and at halftime we were only up by six points when we should have had the game salted by then."

"We went down to the coach's room, and Mr. Donohue started picking us apart and telling us how awful we played, and then he pointed to me and said, 'And you! You go out there and you don't hustle. You don't move. You don't do any of the things you're supposed to do. You're acting just like a *nigger!*'

"I haven't the slightest idea what happened in the second half of the game except that I was told I played well and that we won. After the game Mr. Donohue called me into his office and he was all smiling and happy. He put his hand on my shoulder and he said, 'See? It worked! My strategy worked. I knew that if I used that word it'd shock you into a good second half. And it did.' He said a lot more, but all the time I was sitting there with my head hanging down and was thinking, "This is no good, Mr. Donohue! This is no good.' "

When he read the story, Jack Donohue was stunned, surprised, hurt. Yet he remained silent.

"What good would it have done to say anything?" he asked, rhetorically. "It would only have prolonged an unpleasant situation. What good would denials be? Anybody who knows me knows I couldn't have said that. No, I'm not angry with Lewie. That incident was supposed to have happened when he was a junior. That's a long time ago. His memory may be at fault or maybe he misunderstood something I said.

"We talked many times, for long periods of time, and that word came up often in our talks. He asked me what I thought of that word and I said I thought nothing of it. It wasn't worth thinking about and people who used it weren't worth thinking about. I tried to impress upon him that if he didn't play up to his ability, if he took the easy way out, if he didn't work hard, people would call him that.

" 'I don't want people to call you that name,' I said. 'Don't let some of those jerks call you that name. You're too good for that.' I tried appealing to his pride. When we talked, when that word came up, I was never downgrading him. I would never think of doing that. I figured that was my job as his high school coach, just as it was my job to protect him from outsiders. I told him, 'People don't want you for yourself, but because you're a basketball player.' I did what I could for him while I was his coach. When he goes to college, I figured, he will have another coach and my job will be done.

"We talked often about what he was going to have to go through. One time he came to me very depressed and hurt. He said he and another black kid on the team, Eric Brown, had been to this school dance and Eric asked a girl to dance, a white girl, and she refused him. Lewie couldn't understand that. He couldn't understand why she would refuse him just because Eric was black.

"We talked about it for more than two hours. I said, 'Lewie, you don't know she refused him just because he's black. Now, I'll admit, it's likely that was the reason, but you don't know for sure. Maybe there were other things about Eric she didn't like. A lot of girls have refused to dance with me and I'm not black.'"

And there was Alcindor saying, in the *Sports Illustrated* article, that he resented going to Friendship Farm.

"He never told me that," Donohue said. "If he felt that way, he should have told me. Every 15 or 16-year-old does a lot of things he doesn't want to do, but people have to force them to do what's best for them, with their best interests at heart. What he's doing is dropping his parents out of it. If he's not old enough to say no, his parents are. Lewie has very substantial parents. He wasn't from a broken home, it wasn't that he had parents that didn't care. His parents are concerned and intelligent people. If they thought these things were wrong, they could have stopped them. Didn't he think of that?

"I'm not bitter, but I'm confused," Donohue said. "I knew him very well. We spent a lot of time together in four years. You get to know somebody when you spend that much time with him. I haven't talked to him in four years, but I can't believe he's changed that much."

But Lew Alcindor had changed. The people around him had changed. His circumstances had changed. He had matured, he had struck out on his own. Lew Alcindor had changed and there was no turning back.

4

HIGH SCHOOL

The weekly meeting of the Chicago Basketball Writers Association had come to order. On his feet was the guest speaker of the week, Ken Norton, coach of Manhattan College. He had come all the way from New York to help publicize his school's game against Northwestern University in the Chicago Stadium.

But Norton chose not to talk about the Manhattan-Northwestern game. He chose to talk about something else, something that would be of more universal interest. He chose to talk about recruiting, in general, and one high school player in particular.

"Maybe I shouldn't tell you about him," Ken Norton said to an audience that was made up, in part, of at least a dozen college coaches. "Maybe I should keep this to myself, but, well, there really are no secrets and you'll hear about him soon enough anyway. There's a kid in New York, a sophomore at Power, who's going to be the greatest player in the game. He's only 15 and already he's seven feet tall and doctors say he's still growing. His name's Alcindor."

"Will you repeat the name?" asked a reporter in the rear of the room. "Is it Al Sindor—S__I__N__D__O__R—and is the school Powell?"

"No, no," corrected Ed Hickey, Marquette coach. "It's Power. When we played St. John's in Madison Square Garden, we worked out in the Power gym. They had the tallest ball boy we've ever seen. His name is Alcindor . . . Spanish name."

"I know the boy," said George Ireland, coach of Loyola of Chicago. "What's his first name? I've forgotten."

"It's Ferdinand Lewis Alcindor, Junior," put in Vince Cazzetta of Seattle University, "and George, you must be kidding. You had six New Yorkers on your varsity and freshman teams

43

last season. You scout New York basketball pretty good."

The smile that spread across George Ireland's face betrayed his feigned ignorance. Lew Alcindor had played one unimpressive season of varsity ball in high school and already his reputation had spread across the land. It wasn't easy to overlook a boy who stood seven feet tall by the time he was a sophomore in high school.

When he entered his sophomore year, Alcindor hit exactly seven feet, one-quarter of an inch on Jack Donohue's tape measure. He weighed 220 pounds, wore a size 16D sneaker and slept in a seven foot, six-inch bed. He had grown an inch and a half since his freshman season, but that was not the only change in Lew Alcindor.

With a year of varsity experience behind him and the confidence and improvement that came with that year of experience, Alcindor was ready to do his stuff for Power Memorial as a sophomore. It was a very good year. Lew used his height to pull down 444 rebounds, an average of 16 a game, and he worked to improve his shooting and scored 515 points, a 19.1 average.

Dononue got him to work close to the basket

and to use his exceptional body to great advantage, leaning into the basket and holding the ball in his large, outstretched hand. His greatest weapon was a short hook shot, which he could shoot just as well with his left hand as he could with his right hand, which was the natural way.

He made 53 percent of his shots from the floor and Power won 27 games without losing and walked off with the first of three straight New York City Catholic high school championships. Lew was named to the All-American high school team for the first of three straight times. About the only part of his game that was weak was his foul shooting. Alcindor shot only 66 percent from the line, the better to encourage comparison with Wilt Chamberlain.

Comparisons are inevitable in sports, and already, basketball people were stacking Alcindor against Chamberlain, the natural yardstick. "Better than Chamberlain at comparable stages in their careers," was the consensus on Alcindor. Lew did not mind the comparison. Chamberlain had always been his model.

"I used to shoot like him, comb my hair like him, the whole bit," he said recently.

Perhaps there is a tendency to exaggerate when comparing athletes of different decades.

Perhaps there is a tendency to forget the past. Two years later, Chamberlain was to see—and compare—for himself.

The San Francisco Warriors were playing the New York Knickerbockers in Madison Square Garden and Wilt arrived early, in time to watch the first half of the high scool preliminary game, Power Memorial vs. Archbishop Stepinac. It was Wilt's first look at Alcindor in competition and he was impressed. Lew had scored 15 points in the half as Power had taken a 30-19 lead.

"I think he's the greatest high school player I ever saw," said the man who had been considered the greatest high school player a lot of people ever saw when he played at Philadelphia's Overbrook High.

An indication of how frustrating it was to play against Alcindor in high school is evidenced by an incident that occurred during a pre-season scrimmage with perenially powerful Boys High of Brooklyn. Unable to stop Lew, the Boys High player guarding him finally found a way. He bit Lew on the arm. It stopped Alcindor, but only momentarily and quite illegally. Playing by the rules, there was no way to stop him.

The legend of Lew Alcindor continued to

grow in his junior year at Power. There was no stopping him, no coping with his immense size, and as he continued to improve, defensing him was impossible. It was like watching a man playing with children as opponents who barely reached up to his shoulders waved futilely at Lew in a vain attempt to stop him from scoring or rebounding. He could have scored 60 points a game any time he wanted to, but Donohue would not permit it. In most games, Alcindor played little more than a half. And when he was on the court, coach Donohue's training was evident. Lew Alcindor played not for Lew Alcindor, he played for his team, as part of the team. Winning came first for Lew Alcindor, a characteristic he maintained long after he left Power Memorial.

His junior year was another super-sensational year for Lew, another unbeaten year, another year of being named All-America, of leading his team to a city championship, of being written up in all the New York papers as basketball's next superstar, of being inundated with letters and telephone calls from college coaches, scouts and just hangers-on. He averaged 26 points, 18 rebounds and 22 letters and telephone calls a game as Power ran its unbeaten streak to 52 games, one short of the New York City record.

The highlight of the season came in January. The team had been invited to travel to the University of Maryland Fieldhouse in Hyattsville, Md., to play a game against DeMatha High School of Washington, D.C., an intra-city match of high school basketball powers. What Power Memorial was to New York, DeMatha was to the Washington-Maryland area, a powerhouse team, a school that consistently turned out winning records and outstanding players. Like Power, DeMatha was unbeaten when the two schools met

There were 14,000 people in the fieldhouse for the game, and looking around, you'd have to believe that 13,000 of them were college coaches or scouts. Power won the game, 65-62, won it because Alcindor came alive in the second half. He scored 35 points and grabbed 21 rebounds for the game, a truly superlative effort against such a tough opponent.

By Alcindor's senior year, the recruiters were working overtime to find some link to Lew. The requests for permission to talk to him, which had started as a trickle in his sophomore year, were now a steady flow. The coach of one Far West school carried on regular correspondence with Jack Donohue for three years. Lew had just concluded his sophomore season when the letters began arriving:

May 31—"As I told you, we are permitted according to NCAA regulations to furnish Lew with a round-trip ticket that includes a 48-hour visit on campus. During this time, he would meet our coaches . . ."

June 7—"I think you have made a sound decision to hold off Lew's trip until his junior or senior year. Just let us know when he is ready."

November 4—"I will be in New York on November 12 . . . and I would appreciate the opportunity of meeting you and Lew."

On November 12, Donohue met with the coach, alone, in his office at Power Memorial.

"Jack," said Mr. Anxious Coach, "I'd like Lew to have dinner with [and here the coach mentioned a famous name]. He's one of our most famous alumni. He wants to tell Lew how much he'll enjoy our school."

Donohue was firm: "The rule is this," he said. "No talking to Lew until his senior year."

Alcindor's senior year had come and, with it, an avalanche of requests for meetings, dinners, talks, anything. Filtering the calls and letters was a full-time job but Donohue had committed himself and he was determined to see it through.

Several Southern schools wrote to Donohue saying they were ready to break their color line with the right player. Such a player would have to be intelligent, have strong moral fiber and be a good enough player to insure success. And, it would help if he happened to stand seven feet tall.

Lew had offers from hundreds of schools. He could have gone to any college in the country. Not that it would ever have become a problem, but, for the record, he maintained at Power a scholastic average in the low 90s and high 80s which kept him in the upper 10 percent of his class.

From Maryland University, coach Bud Millikan wrote: "We are fully aware of how sought-after this young man will be."

From Boston College, Bob Cousy wrote: "We are in the process of building a solid basketball program and hope you may become a part of it."

From Oklahoma University, coach Bob Stevens wrote: "All that we ask is an opportunity to talk to the boy."

Representatives of several colleges wrote to Donohue with a thinly-camouflaged suggestion that their school was in search of a new coach and that Donohue might be the man for the job—if he could bring Alcindor along with him. Although he was anxious to advance from high school coaching to a more lucrative and more prestigious college job, Jack refused to be a party to such schemes. The height of bad taste came from the influential alumnus of one midwestern college.

"Our coach underwent surgery recently," wrote this great humanitarian, "and I'm very sorry to say I believe he does not have long to live. He's a very close friend of mine and it saddens me to write this. I visited him just the other day and his condition is rapidly deteriorating. I doubt if he will last the year . . . I thought if you have a friend who is a good coach, it would pay to apply for the job . . ."

This letter Jack Donohue tossed into the waste basket in disgust.

The high point of Alcindor's senior season was a second trip to Hyattsville, Md., and a return match with DeMatha. Again the University of Maryland Fieldhouse was filled to capacity for this high school game of the year.

Entering the season, Donohue had been concerned. Art Kenney had graduated and Donohue was disturbed by his team's lack of height—with the exception of Lew—and with its lack of outside shooting.

"I thought we might lose a few games that year," Donohue said. But, coming into the De-Matha game, Power had increased its winning streak to 71 straight. Alcindor had not played in a losing game since his freshman season.

DeMatha had won 23 straight with a team that had two 6-8 players, Bob Whitmore and Sid Catlett, both of whom went on to play at Notre Dame, and Bernie Williams, a backcourt star who went to LaSalle College, then became an outstanding pro guard for the San Diego Rockets of the NBA.

Their second game was almost a replica of the first, a close, hard-fought struggle. DeMatha played two men on Alcindor, Whitmore in front of him and Catlett in back, and frustrated Power's efforts to get the ball into the big pivot man. Unable to get the ball to Lew, Power was forced to shoot from outside, with little success. Alcindor scored only 16 points and when DeMatha grabbed a lead, it slowed the game down, protecting its lead, and won the game 46-43.

Power's streak had come to an end after 71 straight victories. Lew Alcindor had played on the losing side for the first time since he was a

14-year-old freshman. Lew's parents had made the trip from New York and as they waited for their son to dress and meet them for the long ride home, tears of disappointment streamed down the face of Mrs. Alcindor.

In the Power dressing room, the gloom was as thick as a London fog. Several players cried and, for a long time, Alcindor sat in front of his locker, still dressed in his uniform, his head in his hands, mumbling to himself, blaming himself for the defeat because he had scored only 16 points.

"Now wait a minute," Donohue said, interrupting the gloom. "It's very selfish of you to say you lost this game. What you're implying is that you won all the other games. If you want to take the blame for losing this game, then you have to take credit for winning the other 71. Are you willing to take credit for them? Yes or no?"

Donohue was using a bit of coaching psychology to snap Lew out of his disappointment. No, Lew said, he was not willing to take credit for winning the first 71 games.

"I'm the coach and I'm not blaming myself for losing this game," Donohue added. "If I did, then I'd be taking credit for winning all the others and I'm not going to do that because it's not true."

—The DeMatha game was to be the last time Lew Alcindor would play on the losing side in high school, the only game he would lose out of 79 in his last three high school seasons. Power went on to win its third straight CHSAA championship, Lew being named to the high school All-America team for the third consecutive time.

In his last high school game on March 8, 1965, Power defeated Rice High School, 73-41, for the championship. Lew had entered the game needing 28 points to tie the all-time New York City scoring record. He scored 32, took 22 rebounds and blocked eight shots. He finished his career with 2,067 points and 2,002 rebounds, both New York City records.

It was over. Lew Alcindor had played his last game as a schoolboy and it was over. But it still wasn't over, really. Not yet. There was still the decision to be made. At the time, there were six newspapers in New York City and each day at least one of them ran an "exclusive story" announcing Alcindor's future plans.

He was going to become the first black basketball player at North Carolina; he and Donohue were going to Dayton in a package deal;

he had decided on the Ivy League and was trying to make up his mind between Yale, Harvard and Princeton; he was all set for UCLA; St. John's had him locked up; he would forego college and sign a million-dollar contract to play with the Harlem Globetrotters; the NBA would make an exception and take him into the league right out of high school.

That last far-fetched tale came about after Gene Shue, coach of the Baltimore Bullets, said: "I'll trade two first round draft choices for him right now," and someone wrote a story pointing out that there was no reason Lew could not step right into the NBA.

There was an NBA rule, the story said, that a player could not leave college and sign with an NBA team until his class had graduated. "But," the story continued, "if that player never goes to college, he has no class and he does not have to wait."

If Lew had been permitted to speak to the press, he would have told them that he had every intention of going to college and getting his degree.

Meanwhile, he had narrowed his choice down to five—UCLA, Michigan, Boston College, St. John's and NYU.

National champions for two straight years,

UCLA was making a big push to land Alcindor. There was a letter to Lew from Dr. Ralph Bunche pointing out the advantages of the California school, where Dr. Bunche had played varsity basketball in the 1920s.

Willie Naulls, a UCLA alumnus then with the Boston Celtics of the NBA, spent hours with Lew extolling the blessings of his alma mater.

There were stories that Jackie Robinson, another UCLA alumnus, had contacted Alcindor to make a pitch for the Trojans; and that Sammy Davis, Jr., had met with Lew in New York and entertained him at dinner, all the while trying to convince him that UCLA was the place for him.

In April of his final year at Power, Lew flew to California to visit the campus of UCLA. He was met at the airport by Edgar Lacey, a junior and one of the Trojans' star basketball players. Lacey took young Alcindor under his wing and showed him around the campus. Alcindor met briefly with coach John Wooden and found him to be a pleasant, soft-spoken, kind man, who seemed more like the corner druggist than the coach of the finest team in college basketball.

Lew took a liking to Wooden and came away from his visit with the feeling that he had not been high pressured at UCLA. If he wanted to go to school there, he would be welcome. If he wanted to go elsewhere, his decision would be respected. Lew left California impressed with Wooden and with UCLA and excited about the idea of joining the team that had won the national championship that year.

But there was still a great deal of pressure from his parents for Lew to go to a New York school. St. John's was still very much in the picture and NYU was making a belated, but powerful, push. At either of these schools, Lew's parents could see their boy play most of his games in college. As most parents would be, they were unhappy at the thought of their boy going to a school 3,000 miles away from home.

While Alcindor was visiting campuses, trying to make his decision, another complication arose. Jack Donohue had been hired to take over as basketball coach at Holy Cross college and there was speculation in the newspapers that Alcindor would follow his high school coach to Holy Cross as a package deal. It was nonsense for two reasons. Alcindor had long decided the last place he would go to college was where Jack Donohue was coach. And Donohue had accepted the offer from Holy Cross on the condition that the job was not contingent upon his delivering Alcindor.

Once convinced that Holy Cross wanted him for himself and not for Alcindor, Donohue accepted the job and tried to get Alcindor to go along with him.

"As a college coach," he explained, "I'd be a fool if I didn't try to recruit the greatest high school player in the country."

Several times, Donohue asked Alcindor to take a trip to Worcester, Mass., to look over the Holy Cross campus and each time Lew declined. "What good would it do?" he asked. "I'm not going to go there anyway."

Finally, out of loyalty, Lew decided he owed his high school coach the courtesy of a visit to Holy Cross.

"I don't think it will change my mind," he said, "but if you really want me to visit, I will."

"I said yes, I wanted him to visit," Donohue recalls. "I really believed I had a chance to get him. He visited the campus and said he was surprised. He said he never realized Holy Cross was as nice as it is. But I believe he had already made up his mind by then."

Alcindor had made up his mind and, with the help of Jack Donohue, he was about to announce his decision to a waiting world. It was

Donohue's suggestion that the announcement should come as soon as possible, to put an end to all the wild and silly speculation, and that it should be done formally, at a press conference, to give all concerned an equal chance at the story.

The press conference was called for 12:30 on the afternoon of Tuesday, May 4, 1965. More than 80 members of the press, radio and television were on hand and the crowd amazed Donohue.

"I didn't realize this many people would be interested in this," he said. "I don't even know who told most of them about it. I only called a few people. I don't think Lewis realized how big it would be."

The meeting was held, fittingly, in the Power Memorial gymnasium. On the walls of the gym were more than a dozen banners heralding Power Memorial as champion of tournaments in Providence and Schenectady, as national high school champions, as champion of their league, the Catholic High Schools Athletic Association, all but two of the banners having been earned since Alcindor arrived at Power.

While the press conference was going on, the Power Memorial Parents Association, was decorating the gym for a dance that was to be held that night. Among the mothers working on the decorations was Mrs. Cora Alcindor.

At 12:33 p.m, Alcindor arrived, ducking his head through the doorway to enter the room. He walked slowly, but purposefully, to the center of the gymnasium where a microphone had been placed. The microphone had been drawn out to its fullest height so that it swayed and tottered like a straw in the wind. Lew stood at the microphone, looking at Jack Donohue and rubbing his hands together for almost a minute until Donohue nodded for him to speak and he spoke.

His voice was soft and deep and steady and what he had to say was brief and to the point. He did not read from a prepared statement, but as the words came out, it was obvious he had gone over several times in his mind what he would say.

"This fall, I'll be attending UCLA in Los Angeles. That's the decision I came to. It has everything I want in a school."

And so, just like that, it was done. The decision had been made. Only time would tell if it had been the right one.

5

FRESHMAN

California beckoned, all sunny and golden, a land of hopes, a land of dreams, a land of bronzed Adonises and sun-bleached blondes and upturned noses, a land of fantasies and make believe, a land of phonies.

"I didn't unpack my bags for a week," Lew Alcindor remembers, "I was so homesick."

Starting college is a difficult adjustment for an 18-year-old under normal conditions. Lew Alcindor was not starting college under normal conditions. He was seven feet, two inches tall, he was black, he was 3,000 miles from home. He had come to California to play basketball.

He had come with a reputation that was nation-wide, a reputation of being potentially the greatest basketball player ever to play the game. His fellow students at UCLA thought of him not as a person, a confused and lonesome teenager; they thought of him as a tall, black, point-making machine.

He had fallen in with his own little clique. He had been befriended by Edgar Lacey, a junior and a star on the varsity basketball team. And he had his own group of buddies, all living in Dykstra Hall, the dormitory where UCLA's athletes were housed. Fortunately, if you are a basketball player, you do not have to wait long to do the thing you have been brought to college to do. And Lew Alcindor did not have to wait long to begin playing basketball, to get out there on the basketball court where he belonged, where he felt at home.

Basketball practice began in November and now Lew was no longer homesick. Now he was doing the thing that was familiar to him, the thing that he had done every year for the last eight years. On November 27, Alcindor put it out there for all to see. The UCLA freshmen met the UCLA varsity, the first pre-season game, California's first look at Lew Alcindor in competition. It was a game that filled the

Pauley Pavilion, UCLA's new gymnasium that, not coincidentally, was dedicated with Alcindor's first game.

The Bruins had won two straight national championships and they were rated No. 1 in the country in all pre-season polls but Alcindor and his freshman teammates put on a devastating display of power and talent. They beat the varsity, 75-60, with Lew scoring 31 points. It was awesome. It was frightening. Alcindor was only 18 years old.

"He could play in the NBA right now," said Fred Schaus, general manager of the Los Angeles Lakers.

"UCLA" wrote one newsman, "is No. 1 in the country and No. 2 on its campus."

Even basketball was not fun for Alcindor in his freshman year. There was less competition than there had been in high school. He played against teams like the Pepperdine freshmen, Palomar Junior College, San Diego Community College and Orange Coast College. The UCLA freshmen beat Citrus Junior college by 103 points.

Coach John Wooden had put together a fantastic freshman cast to go along with Alcindor. There were four other high school All-Americas on the squad—6-4 Kenny Heitz from Santa

Maria, California; 6-4 Kent Taylor from Houston, Texas; 6-5 Lynn Shackleford, an amazing left-handed outside shooter from Burbank California; and Lucius Allen, a 6-2 guard with pro moves and blazing speed, from Kansas City, Missouri, who was Alcindor's roommate at Dykstra Hall.

Alcindor derived more fun, more experience, more value and more satisfaction out of practice sessions than he did in those lopsided freshman games.

Wooden had recruited another big man shortly after Alcindor arrived. He brought in Jay Carty, a six-foot, eight inch graduate student from Oregon State. Carty had starred at Oregon State and coached its freshman squad, where his pet project was seven-footer Mel Counts. Wooden made Carty assistant freshman coach with instructions to concentrate on the tutoring of Alcindor. Carty's job was to teach by doing, to provide the competition in practice that Alcindor was not getting in freshman games.

He took on Lew one-on-one in practice and the two went at it by the hour, Carty making moves on Alcindor to improve the young man's defense and giving him a physical workout to improve Lew's toughness and give him a hint of what lay before him when he moved up to the varsity. Carty used all the tricks, a well-placed elbow, a knee, a hip. He drew a line on the backboard 18 inches above the rim and instructed Lew to jump up and touch the line 20 times, 10 with each hand, every day.

"He thought basketball was too easy," Carty explained, "and I found it hard to condemn him since the team was doing so well and he was doing so well. But I found that Lew really responds to authority. He worked hard and never protested."

It wasn't authority that was responsible for Lew's response. It was pride and determination and the strong desire to be a winner, to be the best player there is.

In little time, Alcindor became one of southern California's leading tourist attractions, right up there with Disneyland, the Farmer's Market, Sunset Strip and Hollywood and Vine.

Freshman games were outdrawing the varsity at Pauley Pavilion and tiny gyms were filled to capacity when the UCLA freshman team played on the road in suburban Los Angeles.

It was Friday night in Fullerton, a night not unlike any other Friday night in any other town in suburban America. The juke joints worked overtime and there was a big run on the drive-ins and some of the kids made it to the basketball game.

But this Friday night was unlike any other in Fullerton. This Friday night Lew Alcindor was playing in Fullerton. You know, the big kid from New York. Let's go to the game and see if he's any good.

So they came to the sparkling new gym which seats 4,300 and rarely is even half filled, but on this Friday night the gym was crowded to overflowing. They came for the same reason you would come to see Jo-Jo the Dog-Faced Boy or Matilda the Fat Lady or Igor the Sword Swallower. They came to snicker and sneer and gawk at this unusually tall young man who would like to run and hide from the snickers and sneers but knows he cannot.

When they introduced him, it was not "Lew Alcindor of UCLA" it was "Lew Alcindor, seven feet, one and one-half inches" and they introduced him right after Lucius Allen, who is 6-2, and Lew Alcindor had to run out on the court with all those eyes glaring at him and he had to stand next to Lucius Allen and listen to the crowd buzz and snicker and laugh.

He lined up for the center tap against a boy from Cal State Fullerton and the boy's name was Steve Ball and he stood 6-3 and there were more snickers. They giggled when he spread the tentacles he uses for arms and waved his huge hands in the face of a pygmy opponent vainly trying to shoot the ball and when he leaped into the air and came down with an earth-shattering thud, the ball stuck in his hand like an orange, and they howled when he turned and rammed the orange into the basket with a kind of defiance.

This was not a basketball game, it was an exhibition and Lew Alcindor was the main attraction. He was Jo-Jo the Dog-Faced Boy and Matilda the Fat Lady and Igor the Sword Swallower and when the game was over the young Richard Chamberlains left arm-in-arm with the young Doris Days and they would talk into the night about the fantastic giant as if he was something from another planet, something to be held in awe and fear.

He had given them their money's worth in entertainment. They had come to laugh at him and they had laughed, but for some it was not enough. For some, it is never enough. He had showered and dressed and he was walking out of the gym toward the bus that would take him back to the dormitory and his books, when a man approached him.

"Hey, kid, how tall are you?"

No answer.

"Hey, you, I said how tall are you?"

Still no answer.

"Fresh New York punk."

"I ignored him," Alcindor said later, "because he was rude. What difference could it possibly make to him how tall I am? I'm a little over 7-1, I don't even know for sure. How tall am I? Very tall. What possible difference could it have made to that man if I said I was 6-7 or 7-5?"

Alcindor seemed disturbed, preoccupied, unhappy in California. The following day, a sportswriter friend from New York, who had been in Fullerton the night before, called Lew at his dormitory. The conversation went like this:

Friend: "How are you?"

Lew: "Fine."

Friend: "Are you happy here?"

Lew: "Yes I am."

Friend: "You don't sound convincing."

Lew: "Well, final exams are coming up and I'm kind of thinking about them."

Friend: "Can we get together?"

Lew: "If it's for an interview, I'm sorry, but I'll have to say no."

UCLA athletic director, J. D. Morgan, had

placed an impenetrable wall of security around Alcindor. The press was forbidden to interview him.

"It's my rule," Morgan said. "It's been in existence since I become athletic director here. The press is not permitted to talk to any freshman athlete, not only Lew."

Morgan had been at UCLA three years and nobody could remember a similar ban on any other freshman athlete. But, then, nobody could remember another freshman athlete like Lew Alcindor. Lew accepted the dictum without argument. In a way he was relieved because he would have a difficult time studying if he had to comply with all the requests for interviews and portrait-sitting. Yet, something about it was so familiar. It made him think of high school and he had believed that going so far away from home to college would give him certain liberties, would leave him far removed from high school and childhood.

Lew Alcindor seemed disturbed. His friend from New York had noticed a great change in Lew, a change from the young man who had accompanied him to Shea Stadium two months before he was to leave for Los Angeles. Lew was a baseball fan and his favorite team, the Dodgers, were playing the Mets. The friend

69

brought Alcindor on a tour of the Dodger clubhouse and he was awe-struck as he spoke with his baseball heroes, who were just as awed by him.

Willie Davis was friendly: "Call me when you get to L.A. I'd like to have you come to the house for dinner."

Maury Wills was considerate: "I played a little basketball in High School. I'm sure glad I got out before you came along."

Sandy Koufax was kind: "You'll like it in Los Angeles. Good luck to you."

Don Drysdale was interested. "I've read a lot about you. I'm glad you're coming out. I go to the games all the time. I'll be looking forward to seeing you play."

People change and Lew Alcindor had changed in his year away from New York. He was a kid no longer. Now he was an adult, a sensitive, perceptive adult, a thinking, feeling, hurting adult.

It wasn't long before Alcindor began discovering things about California. Strange things. Unreal things.

"I quickly discovered that there is no special breed of people called Californians, with their own culture and background and attitudes. I discovered that most Californians came from other places where racial prejudice abounded, and some of these Californians had the same feelings about race as their friends back home. To these bigoted people, deep down inside, I was nothing but a jive nigger.

"There also seems to be a special art form in California," Alcindor told *Sports Illustrated*. "It's the art of seeming to like people that you really don't like. It wasn't long before I realized that certain cats who hated my guts were giving me the Pepsodent beach boy smile and saying, 'Hello, how are you?' People here have absolutely no commitment to you whatever."

"Lew," said coach John Wooden, "is a bit of an introvert, a bit of a loner. He can be alone in a crowd."

"It's not that he's a moody child," his mother disagreed. "He's not a loner."

She was suggesting that perhaps Lew was homesick and, undoubtedly, that was part of it. He missed his family and his friends and the convenience of travel. In New York he could hop on the subway and go down to Birdland or take a bus to the Apollo Theater in Harlem to dig the sounds, but in California you needed a car and Lew Alcindor, the greatest, most sought-after high school basketball player of his time, did not have a car in his freshman year.

"In New York," he said, "my situation was always a pretty well-defined thing. I went to school, I came home, I played basketball, I had my friends, I went to camp in the summer. Being in California gave me a new perspective. I met new people, discovered new concepts.

"I don't feel lost in California as much as I feel alienated. California runs a game on the rest of the country. It pretends to be liberal, but it is not liberal. Look at what happens in their elections. There are phony people here. I doubt the people are for real here.

"They think I'm moody and reclusive, but under these conditions that's the only way I can be. The people here don't know what's going on around them. I'm disappointed in the atmosphere here. Most of the students seem out of it. They do not know how people in the rest of the world live. They have a limited point of view as opposed to New York City. That is my experience."

Lew learned all about the so-called California liberals on the few occasions when he dated a white girl. Their stares, their remarks told him everything.

"It fences me out, it's so bad," he said. "The

South is in Montgomery, Alabama, but the South is also in Cicero, Illinois; the South is in Great Neck, Long Island; the South is in Orange County, California; it's everywhere."

If he had it to do over, Alcindor said, he might have given more thought to the University of Michigan, but rumors that he would transfer, which came monthly like the electric bill, were totally unfounded. It wasn't the school that disturbed him, it wasn't the campus or the athletic program or his teammates or his coaches.

"The school is great," he said many times. "If they could just transplant the UCLA campus to Times Square. . . . I'm not here to be a social butterfly, just to get an education and the people in the athletic department have been great. They never backed down on one word, on one promise they made to me. If they said they'd do something, they did it. They've kept their part of the bargain and I'll keep mine."

Lew Alcindor's part of the bargain was to play basketball and that's what he did. He averaged 33.1 points and 21.5 rebounds a game for the UCLA freshmen, breaking the school's frosh scoring record by more than 150 points. News of Alcindor's phenomenal freshman season spread across the country, all the way to Holy Cross College in Worcester, Massachusetts.

"I kept telling people I was surprised he did so well after he left me," said Jack Donohue, a rookie coach at Holy Cross. "He was really only 6-2 when he played for me. He just played like he was 7-2."

It was Donohue who had to break the news to the President of Holy Cross that Alcindor had decided to go to UCLA.

"He told me he was just as happy," Donohue recalled, "that it might have been embarrassing. I said I was pretty smart when I coached him in high school and while I agreed that it might have been embarrassing, I could have lived with it."

Instead John Wooden would have to live with the embarrassment and the rest of the coaches on the West Coast would have to live with the problem of Alcindor. They lived in fear. His freshman record had established that.

Alcindor led the UCLA frosh to 21 straight victories and an average of 113.2 points per game to 56.6 for the opposition. From his sophomore year in High School through his freshman season in college, Lew Alcindor had played in 100 games and been on the winning side in 99 of them.

But that was freshman basketball. Varsity basketball could be another story. That remained to be seen, but his freshman year behind him, Lew Alcindor spent a restless summer, an impatient summer, a summer filled with anticipation and anxiety and doubt.

"I can't wait to get started," he told a friend. "Then I can put everything out there for everyone to see."

6

SOPHOMORE

Lew Alcindor's time had come.

"I just wanted to go out there and be able to do my thing and see if it was good enough," he had said. Now his time had come. The night was December 3, 1966, the place was UCLA's jam-packed Pauley Pavilion, the opponent was the University of Southern California, the occasion was Lew Alcindor's varsity debut. The time had come for Lew Alcindor to put it all on the line. All the speculation, all the hard work, all the preparation, all the predictions of great things could not help. Now they would pay off only on results.

For months newspapers and magazines had been filled with stories on the wonder of Lew Alcindor. UCLA was the nation's No. 1 college team and Alcindor was the nation's No. 1 college player in all the pre-season polls. He was expected (not predicted, expected) to lead UCLA to the NCAA championship during each of his three varsity seasons, which, of course, had never been done before. And he had not yet played a varsity game.

"I think a player should have to earn all those things," he said, somewhat annoyed. "I have a chance to earn them, but they should wait until I do something to deserve it. I haven't done anything yet."

But it would not end. His picture appeared on the cover of more magazines than Elizabeth Taylor's. And the burden was on him to produce. If he could not do what they predicted, he would be a failure. If he accomplished all the things they said he would—the three national championships and All-America three straight years—well, what did you expect? He could not win, he could only lose or tie. Few men realize their full potential in life. Lew Alcindor had to realize his full potential just to get a tie.

"Others may take it that way," he said, "I don't. I know one thing, the next three years are not going to be easy . . . especially if you want to win."

But the pressure?

"Pressure can come from anywhere. I expect I'll always have pressure because I set standards for myself that always seem beyond my reach. Anybody can lose. The idea is to make losing a novelty, not a habit. Defeat will not crush me because I have experienced defeat in so many other things, if not in basketball. Music, for instance. I'd love to master a musical instrument. I'm an athlete because that's what I do best and because athletics will be my profession. I'm an artist because that's what I want to do. But lack of time and dedication has made me a failure in that."

That time and that dedication have been studiously applied to basketball and that, as much as his physical endowments, is responsible for his success. He expected the reward to be commensurate with the hard work and dedication and the time spent.

As he warmed up for his varsity debut in Pauley Pavilion, Lew Alcindor's position was already completely defined by the people on the outside looking in. His role in basketball was that he would be the game's most dominant figure over the next decade and a half; that he was expected to deliver three straight NCAA championships to UCLA's Westwood campus; that he would have a greater impact on the game than any player who had come before him; that someday he would be expected to carry a franchise—perhaps an entire league—on his back; that he would become a very wealthy young man the moment he graduates from UCLA and puts his Ferdinand Lewis Alcindor, Jr., on the dotted line of a pro contract.

Most of these things Lew Alcindor acknowledged and accepted without a hint of vanity. He has always been a realist. And while accepting the prejudgments, he also accepted the responsibility, the pressure, the problems and the hard work that would go with them because he is a realist. And yet he had the feeling that some people were going just a bit too far.

"You read some of the things they say and you get scared of yourself," he told a friend. "Like everybody else, I like to see my name in print, but sometimes it can be a drag with all the speculation. I read all these things and I say to myself, 'Is that me they're talking about?' People expect too much, but I'm not impressed with myself as much as some people seem to be. I live with myself and I know I've got shortcomings and I make mistakes ... in life and in basketball.

"People keep telling me I'll be rich someday. They throw around figures like $100,000 and they say they'd love to be in my place. Meanwhile, I'm still as poor as they are. I just wanted to get that first game over with. That way we can stop all the speculation and let the facts speak for themselves. Like we were out there, that was the first game of the season, and it wasn't the kind of pressure that I was trying to prove anything. It was just that it would make it easier for all the talk to end, you know. That was the whole thing."

More than 13,000 had come to see him that first night and a like number had wanted to see him but had been turned away, and Lew Alcindor knew this was it; he knew that he would be judged for a long time on what he did that first night because first impressions are often lasting impressions in sports.

And he put it out there for all to see on that first night. It must have been like this the first time Joe Louis unleashed his lethal left hook on the chin of an opponent. It must have been like this the first time Bob Feller uncorked his fast ball in a game.

Southern Cal had a rookie, too, a rookie

coach named Bob Boyd, who had the unfortunate coincidence of being the first coach to try to stop Alcindor in college. With no precedent to guide him, Boyd decided to play the conventional way—one man guarding Alcindor. It would be the last time in his college career that Alcindor would play without a crowd surrounding him.

Against Southern Cal, Alcindor was superb, as poised as a pro, as graceful as Rudolf Nureyev, as explosive as TNT, as dominant as Moby Dick in your backyard pool. He strode the court like Gulliver in Lilliputia, he intimidated the tiny Trojans with his awesome frame, blocking shots with his long, stringy arms like a man swatting flies. He plucked rebounds like you would pick apples off a tree and moved irrepressibly to the basket to score on driving layups, dunks, short turn-around jump shots and soft, floating hook shots with either hand.

As the first half was coming to an end, the seconds ticking off five . . . four . . . three . . . Mike Warren tossed the ball high toward the hoop—too low for a shot, too high for a pass, it seemed—and Lew Alcindor's long arms stretched to the ceiling and he plucked the ball in his huge hands above the basket and, in one swift motion, jammed the ball down into the net as the buzzer sounded and the Southern Cal players had to know, then and there, that it was a hopeless task they were confronting.

Alcindor was devastating. He put on a frightful display, making 23 of 32 shots from the floor and 10 out of 14 from the foul line as UCLA won, 105-90. In his first varsity game, Lew Alcindor had scored a record 56 points, 14 points more than the previous UCLA record set the year before by Gail Goodrich. Lew Alcindor was as good as advertised. He was better. If this was a portent of things to come, college basketball would be a one-man show for the next three years; no record would be safe from this terrible giant who stood seven feet, one and three-eighths inches tall.

After the game, coach Wooden capsuled Alcindor's performance for reporters with one word. "Awesome," he said. "At times he frightens me."

Next came Duke University, a two-game series with the nation's seventh-ranked team, which would certainly have some idea on how to stop Alcindor. Coach Vic Bubas tried surrounding him with three big men and it worked. It stopped Alcindor, but it didn't stop the Bruins. Lew scored only 19 points. He failed to take a shot for the first seven and a half minutes of the game, preferring to pass the ball to teammates who were open as UCLA won easily, 88-54.

In the second game, Duke played it more loosely against Alcindor with the expected results. The Blue Devils managed to cut the margin by 14 points, but still lost, 107-87, as Alcindor scored 38 points.

"With him in there," Duke coach Bubas said, "you simply can't play your regular brand of basketball. It wouldn't surprise me if he scored 80 points some night."

If he went out to score points, Alcindor probably could have scored at least 80 any night he chose. But he wasn't interested in scoring points or breaking records and, ironically, in three varsity seasons only once—when he scored 61 against Washington State—would he get as many points as he did in his very first game.

"That had all been done before," he said about scoring records. "Frank Selvy once scored 100 points. If I play my games and work hard and we win, they don't have to remember me for setting records. I don't think Bob Cousy ever set any scoring records, but I don't think anybody is going to forget him. Winning is more important to me than setting records."

And win the Bruins did. Playing with three other sophomores and one junior in the starting lineup, Alcindor led UCLA past 21 straight regular season opponents, frustrating every defense rigged especially to stop him. They tried every trick in the book—double teaming, triple teaming, pressing, stalling; and some that were not in the book—elbowing, gouging, bumping, stepping on his feet. Nothing worked.

UCLA won its first 10 games and then the Bruins met the University of California in their eleventh game and the University of California beat Lew Alcindor—they beat him into the ground. Twice they knocked him to the floor and he came off the deck and if he had been knocked down one more time, they would have had to stop the fight.

They pushed, pulled, held, stepped on his feet. They practically stuck their fingers in his eyes. They gouged. They threw big, muscular players at him in waves. Four of them, and they blocked him with all the ferocity of Jerry Kramer and Fuzzy Thurston. Twice they knocked him down, but they could not keep him down.

They punished him in the first half and

UCLA left the floor with a meager three-point lead. With five and a half minutes left, the lead was only 77-71, but it ended 98-78 for UCLA and with Lew Alcindor surrounded by assassins. Alcindor had received a full four-year scholarship at UCLA. They should have given him a paid up policy in Blue Cross.

They bumped him and shoved him, but Alcindor never lost his poise, never changed the stoic expression on his face, never angered, and in the end he had scored 26 points and grabbed 13 rebounds and contributed six assists. They said it was not one of his better games, but they were wrong. It was his best game. He survived.

"Are you bruised?" a newsman asked him after the war.

"Not yet," he said. "Pretty soon, though. It's been like that the past three games. I can't say anything about it, but I don't like it."

He was disturbed. He was not happy with what went on out on the court and he was not happy with himself. "I'm going to have to get stronger because of what's going on," he said. "I get knocked down too much."

It had not been UCLA's type of game. They were not a strong team, not a physical team. They were a team that relied on finesse, on an all-court press and on Lew Alcindor to stay alive.

"There's very little I can do when the game gets like that," Alcindor said. "I try to nullify it by doing something else."

Once he almost lost his cool, but he maintained his composure. That is his style. He must be the intimidator with his play, not the intimidated by physical stuff, and after he picked himself off the floor for the second time, he was angry and he scored the next seven points and turned a six-point UCLA lead into a 13-point lead.

"He always plays his best when it gets tough," John Wooden said, "whenever they're closing in on us. It never does anybody any good to lose his composure. I'm amazed that he can take that kind of play in there and still keep his poise. I think he was irked a little bit. I don't think anybody can handle him legally, but on the other hand..."

On the other hand they were ganging up on him. He was a monster and the only way to stop a monster is to fight dirty and they fought dirty. Anything goes against a monster. But the monster remained unperturbed. His expression did not change. He chewed his gum methodically, incessantly. He played with a bored detachment. And when he was pushed too far, he reacted. He stuffed shots and dominated the game and intimidated anyone who came near his zone on defense. He does not showboat. He just did his job in the face of all the rough stuff.

Wherever he went he was the monster, an ogre that had to be beaten down. The fans were working against him.

"For as long as I can remember," he said, "I've always been the bad guy on the court. I guess I'm slightly whiplashed."

And while the rest of the country stood in awe of Lew, coach Wooden continued to speculate.

"Lewis is still a youngster, emotionally, mentally and in terms of experience," said the soft-spoken, low-key coach. "He's never really been challenged, never really had to drive himself. When that happens, there should be quite an explosion. If he ever puts it all together, operating on defense as he does on offense, he can be truly the best."

Pauley Pavilion was packed whenever he played and when he took his first college road trip, to Seattle to meet the University of Washington, the crowds came out to see him. All 11,100 seats in Washington's Edmundson Pavilion were sold three months before the game, although the Huskies had never before come close to filling the place. Of those 11,100 seats, 5,200 were reserved for student ticket holders, of which there were 14,500, all anxious to see the UCLA wonder.

The school's athletic department resolved the problem this way: Priority went to all students who had witnessed the Huskies' first two games against Iowa and had the punched tickets to prove it.

"We had only 1,700 students at those two games," said John Reid, the school's Sports Information Director, "so we figured they must be our most loyal basketball fans. That's why they got first shot at the tickets."

After that, the remaining student seats went according to seniority—seniors first, then juniors, sophomores and freshmen.

"We figure the freshmen will have two more years to see Alcindor anyway," Reid reasoned.

The second time UCLA met Southern California, the Trojans tried freezing the ball. They held Alcindor to 13, but still lost, 40-35. Oregon also tried the freeze and lost 34-25, with Lew getting 12 points. He was proving that no tactic would work against him, especially those that appealed to his vanity. He gladly sacrificed personal achievements for the good of the team. Wooden did not overlook that characteristic in his star center.

"Lew is exceptionally well-liked by his teammates," he commented. "When he scored 56 points against Southern California, they knew he was supposed to shoot. But when he's bothered, he won't force his shot. Lew will hit all the troubles, I just hope he can compensate. But if his teammates can get the ball into him deep, he'll score. Fundamentally, Lew is a nice boy. He doesn't have all the ideas on defense yet, but he has no mental blocks and he's receptive to teaching. I'd say his high school coach, Jack Donohue, did a tremendous job with the boy. He knows I want no stars. Stars expect too much. Around here, my managers don't go around picking up towels and dirty socks."

UCLA had two games scheduled in Chicago in mid-season, but before leaving Los Angeles, Alcindor got several threatening letters from someone in the Chicago area. There were racial slurs in the letters and they wanted Alcindor not to play in Chicago or he would be shot down on the court. He turned them over to Wooden, who gave them to the FBI, but Alcindor played and the Bruins won both games without incident.

Lew Alcindor was learning what it meant to be a star. And dozens of college coaches around the country were learning the futility of trying to stop him.

"I see no reason why Alcindor won't become the greatest of all time," said De Paul's Ray Meyer.

Howie Dallmar of Stanford saw one consolation: "It's a good thing they outlawed the center jump before he came along or UCLA wouldn't just be winning, they'd be scoring shutouts."

Johnny Dee of Notre Dame: "The only way to beat Alcindor is to hope for the three Fs—Foreign court, Friendly officials and Foul out Alcindor."

Guy Lewis of Houston: "Nothing worked a damn on Alcindor. He peeled us like bananas."

Marv Harshman, Washington State: "He can hold you off with one hand and stuff the ball with the other."

Somebody suggested the only way to beat Alcindor was to legislate against him and get the rules committee to raise the basket.

"The higher they raise it," Alcindor replied, "the farther they move it away from the small man."

On the contrary, said Oregon State coach,

Steve Belko, "I think they should lower the basket to five feet and give everybody an equal chance."

In rebuttal, Alcindor said: "It doesn't matter if you're seven feet or 5-4, the whole challenge is to play well."

"At this stage of the game," said Eddie Gottlieb, former coach and owner of the Philadelphia Warriors, "he's got more coordination than Chamberlain had."

"He's worth as much as the pros can pay," said all-time great George Mikan, a significant comment because Mikan was to become Commissioner of the American Basketball Association.

As Alcindor and UCLA kept mowing down opponents, coaches continued to heap praise upon him, rig defense against him and suggest solutions to keep him from destroying the game.

"Can basketball survive Lew Alcindor?" asked one national magazine.

"Is there a way to beat Alcindor?" asked another, then used 2,000 words to say "No."

Writers wrote reams to extol him and worked overtime to come up with catchy phrases to describe him. He was Mt. Alcindor, the Big A. He played for Lew-CLA or the University of California at Lew Alcindor. When the Bruins played in the NCAA championship tournament, one sportswriter datelined his story, "Lewisville, Kentucky."

In the NCAA tournament, UCLA met the team figured to be its toughest rival, the University of Houston, in the semi-finals. It was billed as a battle of superstars, Alcindor vs. Houston's Elvin Hayes. Alcindor lost the personal duel, being outscored by Hayes, 25-19, and outrebounded 24-20, but, as usual, the Bruins won the game, 73-58, and faced Dayton for the championship.

Preoccupied with stopping Alcindor, the Flyers held him to 20 points, but were shot down by the other Bruins, 79-64.

In his first varsity season, Lew Alcindor had done it all. He had led his team to 30 victories without a defeat and the expected national championship; he had been named to every All-America team; he was the Most Valuable Player of the NCAA tournament; and he had averaged 29.7 points and 15.5 rebounds a game. Lew Alcindor still had two varsity seasons remaining and there were no more worlds to conquer.

7

JUNIOR

The College Basketball Rules Committee had a surprise for Lew Alcindor when he arrived on the UCLA campus for the start of his junior year. He had spent the summer in New York, digging the familiar sights and sounds, getting together with old friends and spending the day hours doing some gratifying work—visiting the city's ghetto areas with professional basketball players Emmette Bryant and Freddie Crawford and giving basketball clinics for the ghetto youth.

When he returned to the UCLA campus for his junior year, they gave him the news. The

Rules Committee had done its bit to stop Lew Alcindor by legislation. From now on, it would be a violation to dunk the ball. It was a strange coincidence. Wilt Chamberlain had come and gone, so had Jerry Lucas, Bill Russell and Oscar Robertson, but there had been no major rules change. Then, the year after Alcindor had cleaned up all the honors in college basketball, they banned the dunk. It would become known as the "Lew Alcindor Rule" and with good reason.

Alcindor took the news philosophically. "I don't like it, but it's not going to hurt my game," he said. "I'll still get my points. If it is a rule against me, they have to realize it's not going to work and they're taking away one of the most exciting plays in the game from the spectator's point of view. I don't like it because it's probably going to mess up the game for the kids in high school."

There may have been another reason for the rule, Alcindor suggested.

"I'm not making any accusations, but if you look at the players who dunk, most of them are black athletes. I don't want to indict anybody, but I bet if you check who's on that Rules Committee, you'll find out some interesting things."

The "no dunk" ban, which many people felt was contrived to keep Alcindor from completely controlling the college game, might have had a reverse effect; it might have been the thing Alcindor needed to give himself new drive. No, he said, his second varsity season was not going to be a hum-drum thing for him. It was not going to be an anti-climax. He had not done it all, there were still new things to do.

"I didn't play to the best of my ability last season," he confessed. "There is room for improvement."

Alcindor improve? The mind boggled at the thought. Opposing coaches shuddered at the prospect. Improve? Where? How?

"My defense," he said. "I still have to work on it. And I have to learn how to handle certain situations, like how to set up a fast break. Learning to throw the ball out when I see it's not going to come back the right way. Knowing when to go back into defense at the right time."

Fundamentals. Always the small things. He stands seven feet, one and three-eighths inches and no man in college basketball is a match for him, yet he is not satisfied with points and victories, with trophies and All-America teams. He would not be satisfied until the day he became the consummate basketball player, a day he said would never come.

"People say there is no challenge left for me after my first year, but I can make my own challenges," he pointed out. "My personal challenge is to improve my game and to keep winning. Everybody will be shooting for us and the challenge is to see that you don't let down. Anybody can have a letdown, either physical or mental. We want to see if we can keep winning. I got the job done last year, but I can do better."

His first varsity season had not been easy for Alcindor, not easy to accept the tactless, unthinking comments about his height. In a Seattle motel, a woman had poked him in the knee with her umbrella to see if he was real and another woman had crept up behind him, shouted "hey" and when Lew turned around, exploded a flashbulb in his eyes.

"I suppose I should get used to being pointed out," he said, "but it's not my nature. It's like being willing to accept insults. Some people can really come up to you and disrespect you a whole lot and you can't let that happen if you're human. You can't let people do things like that."

There had been the controversy of his relationship with the press, the no-talk ban imposed on him in his freshman year, his natural shyness and his lack of time that made him a difficult, if not unwilling, interview. There had been his homesickness for New York and the instances of racial prejudice in progressive California in the year 1967. And there had been the rumors that he would transfer to another school; that he was leaving UCLA to join the Harlem Globetrotters; that he would go off to Europe to play ball; that he would accept 50 percent ownership to turn pro for some ABA team.

He was not completely happy at UCLA, but there was no thought of quitting. He had a job to do.

"I want to get my degree," he said. "Even to switch to another school, I would lose most of my credits and I will lose a lot of time and I'd have to sit out of competition for a year. It's not worth it. I figure as long as I'm healthy, my value will increase. Meanwhile, I will work to improve my game in college."

The early part of his junior year was uneventful for Alcindor. The Bruins continued to win as expected, increasing their winning streak, beating down all opposition with monotonous regularity. The streak had reached 35 ... 40 ... 42 ... 43. Just ahead was January 20 and a much-publicized rematch with the University of Houston, a game that excited the college basketball world. Scheduled for the Houston Astrodome and bringing together the No. 1 and No. 2 ranked college teams in the country, the game was certain to surpass the all-time college attendance record, the 22,822 who watched a doubleheader in Chicago Stadium on February 23, 1946.

It was a big game, big in its national prestige and big to both teams.

"We want to win," Alcindor said, "but I'm not trying to start any big grudge match or anything."

The Houston Cougars were not so blasé however. Still smarting from their defeat to UCLA in the NCAA semi-finals the previous season, the Cougars believed they could beat the No. 1 team. And their star, 6-8 Elvin Hayes, had been openly critical of Alcindor after their game in Louisville.

The tone for their rematch had been set in the game in Louisville. Elvin Hayes is a talker on the basketball court, a stark contrast to the stoic Alcindor, who seems mummified when he plays. Elvin spent the game talking, trying to psych Alcindor.

"Watch this," he would say when he got the

ball close to Alcindor. "We're going to show you how to play this game."

UCLA won the game, but in their personal duel, Hayes got the best of Alcindor, outscoring him and outrebounding him. It meant nothing to Lew.

"I was aware of the rivalry," he said. "We had both collected a lot of publicity during the year. But I didn't go out on the floor with any idea of outdoing Elvin. The idea, as always, was to win."

But their rivalry was a big thing to Hayes. He had outplayed his more heralded opponent and he felt he had earned the right to criticize him. He said his own teammates had "choked" in Louisville and that Alcindor was not all they said he would be.

"He's not aggressive enough on the boards, particularly on offense," Hayes told a gang of reporters in Louisville. "Defensively, he just stands around. He's not at all, you know, all they really put him up to be."

At that moment, Alcindor walked by and teammate Mike Warren shouted, "Hey, Lewis, Elvin wants to see you."

Alcindor went to Hayes and clutched him by the arm and they spoke quietly, then left the arena together. The following afternoon, Alcindor visited Hayes in his hotel room and the two went off to downtown Louisville to shop for a pair of sunglasses for Lew. They stopped at a record shop, where Alcindor picked up a couple of sides by jazz saxophonist Cannonball Adderly and Hayes a record by the Supremes. Later, they returned to Hayes' hotel room to talk basketball for hours.

When he read Hayes' criticism, Alcindor felt betrayed. "I thought we were friends," he said. "I didn't realize until later that Elvin has this big ego thing going. He's entitled to his opinion if that's what he wants to say. I wouldn't have said those things if I were him, but I'm not his conscience and I don't have anything to do with it. If that's how he feels, that's his business. He shouldn't have spoken like that because he lost and everybody saw them lose and it's kind of silly to talk like that when you lose a game. It sounds like sour grapes."

In answer to Hayes' criticism that Alcindor loafs on defense, Lew said: "Sometimes I do relax and sometimes I'm trying to help the other guys out. A lot of times, especially against Houston, some of the bigger guards take Mike Warren, who's only 5-10, and we need help, so I have to drop off my man to help out."

100

That was as far as Alcindor was willing to go in answer to Hayes. The rest he kept to himself; he held it within for almost a year.

"I can't let it upset me," he reasoned, "because when you start getting upset like that, you lose something. You're thinking more about that than you are of winning."

On January 12, in a game against the University of California, Alcindor scratched his left eyeball. With the big game against Houston just eight days away, Lew was suffering from double vision. For three days he lay in bed in a dark room, an eye patch on his injured eye, wondering if he would be able to play against Houston.

Alcindor accompanied the team to Houston, determined to play in the game. There were 52,693 fans in the Astrodome that Saturday night, January 20, a record attendance for a college basketball game, to see No. 1 UCLA, unbeaten in 47 straight games, meet No. 2 Houston, which had won 17 straight since losing to the Bruins in the NCAA semi-finals. And it was carried on 153 television stations from Miami, Florida, to Fairbanks, Alaska.

Alcindor believed his team needed him to continue the winning streak. He suited up and went out to play although his vision had not cleared and he had not worked out for eight days. He missed two games, against Portland and Stanford, which the Bruins won easily without him, and he didn't even shoot baskets for those eight days. The game wasn't five minutes old when Alcindor was gasping for breath and struggling to run up and down the court. He was out of shape for the first time in his basketball life. It was like learning to play the game all over.

Hayes was fantastic. He scored 29 points in the first half as Houston broke on top and led, 46-43, at intermission. UCLA finally drew even at 65-all on Alcindor's basket with 3:01 to play, but field goals by Hayes and Don Chaney gave the Cougars a 69-65 lead with 1:53 to go.

Lucius Allen scored on a drive and was fouled, but he missed the foul shot and Houston held a two-point lead. When Alcindor fouled Ken Spain, Houston had a chance to wrap it up, but Spain missed both foul shots. Then Spain fouled Allen, who made two to tie it at 69-all as Houston inbounded. The ball and Jim Neilsen's elbow reached Hayes almost simultaneously. Foul. Two shots.

The clock had 28 seconds remaining as Hayes stepped to the line with the score tied 69-69. He hit. Then he hit again.

UCLA had the ball out of bounds. Allen passed it to Lynn Shackleford in the corner, but Mike Warren accidentally tipped it out of bounds. Houston's ball.

Chaney passed to Hayes and the Bruins swarmed all over him in a desperation attempt to get the ball back. Elvin dribbled, protecting the ball as he did, then he found guard George Reynolds just over center court. He whipped it to him. Reynolds caught it, dribbled a few times and the buzzer went off as more than 50,-000 fans roared in delight and chanted "We're No. 1."

The fans swarmed down on the field as his Cougar teammates swept Hayes off his feet and carried him off on their shoulders. He had outscored Alcindor, 39-15, had outrebounded him, 15-12, and he had even blocked a shot on his opponent, who was almost six inches taller. It was "the greatest performance I have ever seen in college basketball," according to Houston coach, Guy Lewis. "I wouldn't trade him for two Alcindors."

In victory, Hayes reiterated his remarks of almost a year ago. "I thought Lew couldn't be faked, but this time I faked him out twice. He's a good player, but it doesn't make any difference to me how tall he is."

103

Meanwhile, Alcindor walked dejectedly to the UCLA locker room, a loser for only the second time in 148 games since his sophomore year in high school. He offered no excuses. He said nothing of his injured eye, the double vision, the fact that he was out of shape, but the statistics told it all. He had made only four out of 18 shots from the field. Never before, in 48 varsity games, did he fail to make at least half of his shots from the field.

In the Associated Press and United Press International polls after the game, UCLA was dropped to No. 2 and Houston was elevated to No. 1 and they maintained those positions for the remainder of the season, Houston No. 1 and UCLA No. 2

Lew Alcindor said nothing. His eye healed and he played himself back into shape and UCLA continued to win. He said nothing about the Houston game, but he kept the bitterness and the disappointment within him and he tore a cover off *Sports Illustrated* that showed a picture of Elvin Hayes shooting a basket over his head. He pasted the picture on the inside of his locker to serve as a constant, but not gentle, reminder of that game in Houston. And he kept hoping that the two teams would meet again so that UCLA could avenge that bitter defeat.

Both teams went undefeated through the rest of the season, keeping their rankings and building to a confrontation in the NCAA playoffs.

It came on March 22, 1968, in the Los Angeles Sports Arena. It came in the semi-finals of the NCAA tournament after both teams had survived the early rounds. It came in a head-to-head, eyeball-to-eyeball, national-ranking-to-national-ranking confrontation.

This time, Lew Alcindor was ready. This time, he was in shape and he had no eye injury and he was ready when he felt a nudge in the ribs early in the game and he heard the unmistakable voice of Elvin Hayes say: "Man, we're gonna beat you. We're gonna beat you bad!"

This time it was no contest. UCLA played with a vengeance, holding Hayes to five points in the first half and five in the second half. This time, the Bruins trampled the Houston Cougars, stomped on them, hurt them bad. The final score was 101-69 and it could have been worse except that John Wooden is a man of compassion. The explosiveness of the UCLA offense left Elvin Hayes speechless and it left Guy Lewis limp.

"I feel like a dead man," the Houston coach

said. "That's the greatest exhibition I've ever seen."

And Hayes, so ebullient, so talkative, so ubiquitous in victory, was nowhere to be found in defeat.

"They had a lot to say about us and I don't think they were correct," Alcindor said simply. "They were annoying and insulting. We wanted to teach those people some manners."

Their only defeat avenged, their pride restored, the Bruins could concentrate on nailing down their second straight NCAA title in the "era of Alcindor."

The opposition was the University of North Carolina and it was a breeze. The Tar Heels were no match for Alcindor. They fell behind, 32-22, at the half and never were close. It ended 78-55 with Alcindor getting 34 points and Carolina coach Dean Smith joining the Bruin bandwagon. "This is the best team of all time— and Alcindor is the greatest who ever played college basketball."

In 60 varsity games, Lew Alcindor had been on the winning side 59 times. He had twice been named Most Valuable Player in the NCAA Tournament and he had led UCLA to two consecutive NCAA championships. And he still had one season of competition remaining. Would he and the Bruins make it three for three?

8

OLYMPICS

A country in turmoil; a country on the verge of a racial revolution.

A young man growing up, maturing. A sensitive young man.

A young man in the midst of the revolution. A young man aware of the things going on around him. A young man with feelings and beliefs and pride; pride in himself, pride in his people.

A black young man. A prominent black young man, capable of leading others.

It was inevitable that there would be a clash.

It came in the Summer of 1968, on the eve of the 29th Olympic Games in Mexico City.

The movement was mushrooming, the rumors were stronger than ever. Black athletes were planning to boycott the Olympic Games as a means of pointing up the social injustices that existed in the United States. It was a good idea, but a dangerous one. It was the perfect way to attract attention to The Cause. Black athletes had contributed mightily to the strength of the United States Olympic team all the way back to the time, in 1936, when Jesse Owens won four gold medals in Berlin. He won them with Germany already plotting World War II and he won them in the presence of Adolph Hitler, the Fuhrer of the so-called "master race."

Americans took pride in this humble Negro super athlete, yet the injustices continued. In 1960, Cassius Clay won the Olympic heavyweight boxing championship in Rome, but back in the United States, his Olympic medal draped proudly around his neck, he was denied service at a restaurant.

Something had to be done. A boycott of the Olympics by black athletes was the thing. If white America could treat an Olympic hero like that, they reasoned, then white America could win the Olympics on its own. It was a courageous step; a step that would bring about criticism and ill feeling; a step that would, no doubt, produce an avalanche of hate mail. But it was a step that had to be taken.

The previous fall, on Thanksgiving Day, Harry Edwards, a sociology professor at San Jose State College and a leader of the Olympic boycott, had called a meeting of prominent black athletes on the West Coast for purposes of laying plans for the boycott. Lew Alcindor attended the meeting and that fact became known to the press. The following day, Alcindor granted one of his rare interviews and explained that the proposed boycott was merely in the talking stage, there was not commitment at that time.

"How do you feel about an Olympic boycott?" Alcindor was asked. And he told them. He spelled it all out for them. He nailed the whole thing to the floor.

"Well, if you live in a racist society and you want to express yourself about racism, there's a lot of things you can do and a boycott is one of them."

Whatever the press inferred from that statement, the fact was Alcindor still had not made up his mind to join the boycott—if, indeed, there would be a boycott. He had almost a year to make his decision. He would have to decide the following summer when tryouts for the Olympic team would be held. He could not put aside completely thoughts of the boycott and what he believed to be its necessity, but he was able to store those thoughts deep enough in his mind to concentrate on helping to bring a second national basketball championship to UCLA.

The months that followed were months of deep personal conflict for Lew Alcindor. Ever since he read the life of Malcolm X and began studying Islam, he knew he would become a Muslim. He had been born and raised a Roman Catholic, but, in good conscience, he could no longer embrace the teachings of the Catholic Church. In the summer between his junior and senior years he began taking instructions in Islam. In August he had his shahada (baptism) into Islam. He was a Sunnite Muslim with a new name, Kareem Abdul Jabbar, a new holy book, the Qur'an and a new way of life.

He explained that he could not completely accept the Islam of Muhammad Ali (Cassius Clay and join the Nation of Islam led by Elijah Muhammad.

He told *Sports Illustrated*: "You will never hear me put the knock on another black man— black people already have enough burdens to bear—but let me just say that I found Elijah's religion too narrow, too negative, and in my opinion not truly Muslim at all. The genuine Muslim bears witness that there is one God, that his name is Allah, and that all men—black and white—are brothers. There is no room in Islam for racial hatred of any sort, and I had come to realize that this was exactly the way I felt in my heart. I had worked past the age of rage. I could still become angered at individual acts of hostility and at the whole pattern of racial hostility. But I could no longer believe that the white man was inherently evil and cruel and black men inherently superior, as some of the other blacks are teaching nowadays. That is just the flip side of the old racism. I realized that black was neither best nor worst, it just was; I could no longer hate anybody. I could no longer afford to be a racist. If racism messed up a lot of people who had to take it, then it must also mess up those who had to dish it out. I did not want to be that kind of narrow man.

"I learned that Islam did not judge a man by what he said or what he professed or the number of formal services he attended, but by his acts, and by his acts alone."

The inner conflict in Lew Alcindor extended

112

to other areas. At times he was confused and he showed that confusion by changing his mind often when asked what he would like to do with his life. He talked of going into journalism. He talked of teaching. He talked of music. He talked of photography. At times he seemed dissatisfied with himself.

"Basketball," he once said, "has become mundane for me. It's not as exhilarating when you have to do it. So now I look for other things. First I was writing. About a year ago I got interested in photography. Now it's music."

At the time, he was taking woodwind lessons and that seemed to please him, for a time. "Just playing variations on a simple scale is much more challenging than basketball," he said. "You can never exhaust the possibilities of what you can do in music. I've got this artistic feeling. I'm always looking to do something creative. The people I associate with are artists. I like LeRoi Jones. I once met him in the street and asked him for his autograph. He recognized me. I was surprised."

As a concerned individual, he worries about his people, he fears for the black kids growing up in the ghetto.

"I have a responsibility to them because I'm one of them," he says. "I was born and brought up on 100th Street and Seventh Avenue. These are the guys I grew up with. They're my people. I'm responsible for them."

There are many ways a man can discharge that responsibility and if basketball is Lew Alcindor's way, he will use basketball.

"The kids dig basketball, so they dig me," he says. "They can relate to me, and if I tell them something, they listen. I look at it this way: if I can change 10 would-be junkies into useful citizens, turn them on to school and useful lives, maybe get them started on how to run a crane at four dollars an hour, that's the most important thing I can do right now. Because if each of those 10 turns on another 10 to decent and useful lives, the geometric progression builds up, and pretty soon you can see an end to some of the black suffering that goes on today. That, in my opinion, is where it's at.

"A whole lot of things right now are caught up with this whole idea of image. Like say a certain name and there's a certain image, and I want to try to represent something positive for the people in the community because you know how kids idolize people and it's not good that these idols are something that you wouldn't want your kid to be. So if you take the responsibility on yourself to give him something to

114

look up to, maybe that's one way to encourage them.

"When I was a kid Joe Louis and Jackie Robinson were God. I didn't follow sports completely, but I knew about it. It's important that we start looking out for ourselves because too many times black people are being either looked after paternally or they've been downgraded and we want to end all that so we look out for ourselves. We know what's best for us. You can tell me what to think, but I know what's best for me. I don't want to come and tell you what color to paint your house, so that's really what we want to get going.

"I worry about the kids in the ghetto. I've got to get myself ready. I want to improve conditions for our people. When Jackie Robinson broke in it was enough for him to get base hits because white people thought he wasn't good enough to do it. But it isn't enough anymore. Black intellectuals don't want black athletes for leaders. They feel there have been enough black symbols in sports and jazz. I know that. I'm figuring it out. It's fragmented, man. Some go to church. Some go to school. Some do nothing. Some want revolt. Me? Try to get change as quickly and as painlessly as possible. Try to stand for something positive. Be something positive."

Lew Alcindor is one of the concerned generation of black athletes. It's a good generation, a generation that will accomplish things.

"My generation is starting to do something good," he says. "The generations before this one were confused. Our generation was confused, too, but it is coming out of it. We had to be confused. We were raised with no peace in the world. There's been no peace since I was born. This leads to confusion. My generation is trying to learn something about it. People, young people, are trying to help each other."

And it is because he is trying to help that, while the United States was winning basketball games in Olympic competition in Mexico City, Lew Alcindor believed it was more important for him to be with Emmette Bryant and Freddie Crawford on the streets of Harlem and Bedford-Stuyvesant and Brownsville for something called Operation Sports Rescue, teaching ghetto kids how to play basketball and telling them to stay in school and make men of themselves.

He wasn't needed ·in Mexico City anyway. They had Spencer Haywood, who is 6-9, and

Bill Hosket, who is 6-8, and they won everything in sight even without Lew Alcindor.

When it was time to make his decision on the Olympics, Alcindor said he could not afford to give up a quarter of a semester or two at UCLA. He was maintaining a B-minus average and he was right on schedule to graduate in June of 1969 and he did not want to postpone his graduation. That was his subliminal reason for passing up the Olympics. The real reason was "the atmosphere that it's wrong to represent this country and then have to come back and face the music all over again."

He had made his decision, a decision which, he says, "was one I made myself. I felt I was right, I still feel I was right, and in the same circumstances, I would do the same thing again."

A man, any man, after all, has to do what he thinks is right.

9

SENIOR

Except for a few isolated incidents, the proposed Olympic boycott by black athletes never came off. The United States basketball team, without Lew Alcindor, swept through all its opponents to keep intact its record of never having lost the gold medal. The team's success took much of the heat off Alcindor for passing up the Olympics because, he said, of studies. Now he could concentrate on winding up his collegiate career and look forward to his future as a professional.

Already there was much speculation concerning Alcindor's future as a pro. Would he join the established National Basketball Association? Or would he throw in with the new American Basketball Association? Or would money talk?

"I know there's talk about the two leagues fighting over me," he commented in a rare discussion of his future. "That attention makes me feel pretty good. I don't want to sound money hungry, but I can use that to assure what I'm worth. The rest of the guys will leave here and may make $12,000. I can see six figures immediately and that's a good feeling. If I do get it, I'll invest it and straighten things out for my family. But it is still too far off to think about negotiating with the pros. When I do, I won't have any qualms about talking to anybody. It will be difficult to get drafted by the Knicks [NBA], but I would like New York or someplace nearby like the Nets [ABA]."

All that was far in the future, far enough in the future for Lew to suppress, as best he could, all thoughts of pro ball and the money he would earn at last. His more immediate concern was of his final college season, of trying to win a third consecutive NCAA championship, something no team had ever done.

His senior year was, relatively, a trouble-free year. He felt a unity, a common bond with his

119

teammates that he had not felt in his first three years at UCLA. It was a feeling that comes with knowing you have been through a lot together. Certainly, they had experienced pressure, the pressure of knowing they had to win, were expected to win all the time. And there was the boredom that comes with winning easily, methodically. All athletes need a challenge and UCLA had put down so many challenges there seemed to be none remaining.

One player expressed it this way: "What we really need is a good scare. We've won so much and so easily the past few years that we don't get keyed up for very many games."

There was within Lew Alcindor a kind of exhilaration that he had almost come through all the pressure, all the crises and in just a few months it would be over and he would be his own man.

"I feel a big relief," he admitted. "I can see the light at the end of the tunnel. I'll get my degree soon and be finished with this whole academic scene forever. I guess the studies, basketball and the people always around finally got to me. Now all I worry about is winning all our games if we can."

There was even time for some fun in his senior year. The Bruins had been invited to compete in the annual Holiday Festival Tournament in Madison Square Garden and it meant Lew could spend Christmas week at home, with his parents and friends. He had played in New York the year before, against Boston College and against Holy Cross and his old high school coach, Jack Donohue. But it was different then. The burden to prove himself in his first appearance in New York as a collegian was too great and it was only a two-day visit, not enough time to see the people he wanted to see and do the things he wanted to do.

The Bruins' first tournament game was against Providence. It wasn't one of their better games, but it was good enough. With UCLA it almost always is good enough. Even on their bad nights, there was enough Bruin power to beat most teams and there was Alcindor, intimidating, irrepressible as always. UCLA won, 98-81 and Lew scored 26 points and acted like he never heard the boos and remarks that came from the stands in this, his home town. But teammate Kenny Heitz heard them.

"We expect it now," said Heitz, a bespectacled forward who was known as the team intellectual and who had been with Alcindor since their freshman days. "Anywhere we play, we get the same kind of racist crap. There was

121

some fat guy here today who kept yelling things at Lew from the stands and you could tell what he was.

"You should read some of the letters Lew gets from racists because he didn't go to the Olympics. I've gotten a letter myself from North Carolina somewhere, asking how I can play with that nigger. I suppose I should try to be unaffected by it, but I feel you should judge a man as a man and that's that."

The following night, North Carolina, nationally ranked and judged to be UCLA's toughest opposition for the Holiday Festival championship, played against Villanova. All members of the UCLA team were invited to see the game, but it was optional and only Curtis Rowe and Sidney Wicks attended. Alcindor took the opportunity to visit with friends and listen to some jazz.

"Coach doesn't believe in scouting," Wicks pointed out. "We just play our game and let the other team make the adjustments."

It is a luxury a player like Alcindor affords a coach. And the following night, Lew showed why. Princeton was no match for him. UCLA won, 83-67, and Alcindor scored 40 points. It should have been hailed as a spectacular performance and it was, by most. The press, the capacity Garden fans. Only UCLA coach John Wooden was unimpressed. He was, to put it bluntly, openly disturbed.

"I think Lewis was far more lackadaisical on defense tonight than he's ever been," Wooden said critically. "In fact, I don't think he's played well on this trip."

Perhaps Wooden was spoiled by Alcindor. Yet, he was the one man who would know when Lew was not playing up to his capabilities and points did not influence him. They never did.

In the final game, UCLA met St. John's, a Cinderella team in the tournament and, quite naturally, the home town favorite. The Redmen made it close for awhile. They were tied, 11-11, after 10 minutes, as close as 31-27 at halftime and 41-37 almost midway into the second half. Then Alcindor went to work and when Alcindor goes to work it is like a raging flood overtaking a tiny town. UCLA won, 74-56, and Alcindor had scored 30 points, collected 22 rebounds and picked up the tournament's Most Valuable Player trophy to add to his ever-growing collection of hardware.

"To get beaten, they'd have to be hypnotized . . . medicated . . . drugged," said St. John's coach, Lou Carnesecca.

Meanwhile, Carnesecca's predecessor at St.

John's, Joe Lapchick, one of the most respected men in the basketball business, was adding his thoughts. "I don't think there's any question about it," Lapchick said. "Speaking strictly in terms of dollars and cents, Alcindor will get more than anybody else past or present."

Is he, Lapchick was asked, the greatest player in basketball history?

The veteran coach thought back over 50 years of basketball and tempered his enthusiasm with caution. "I'll just say he's potentially the greatest."

Nearby, Alcindor, pleased with himself, happy to have played so well at home, satisfied with his performance and obviously at peace with himself for the first time in a long time, was signing autographs for a small army of admiring kids. Patiently he scribbled as the young people clustered around, clutching their pieces of paper and programs and autograph books in their hands and raising up on tip toes to reach him.

"Watch him," said teammate Lynn Shackleford. "He'll sign for all the kids first and ignore the adults. That's one thing that turns Lew on—children. I think that's what he really looks forward to, having children of his own."

It was a rare scene. At times, he was not so

easily approached. At times he seemed to want to be off alone somewhere. Once he said he longed for "some island, some place to get away from it all."

At other times, he was more outgoing. He even made one of his infrequent public appearances to see a basketball game. It was a special basketball game, the Boston Celtics vs. the Los Angeles Lakers. But Alcindor was interested in a duel within the game, Bill Russell vs. Wilt Chamberlain. Here, in head-to-head competition, were professional basketball's two leading centers, the two centers who would provide the toughest opposition for Alcindor if he chose the NBA. There was much speculation on how Lew would do against Russell and Chamberlain and now Alcindor allowed himself to join in the speculation.

"My only worry," he said, "is getting beat up. And I mean getting beat up all the time. I watched only the NBA so far and it's incredible. I don't know if I'm strong enough. But Bill Russell is built like me and he's doing it, so maybe . . .

"Officials could stop all the pushing and shoving under the board. I know fans who like finesse, an Elgin Bayler or a Gus Johnson. I don't enjoy a pushing game. I know I'll get shoved around a lot and I don't know what I'll do about it. I could start a weight program like Wilt, but I've watched him and he didn't impress me as the most agile. He's so strong, he just pushes his way to the basket and makes those hooks."

The remarks were a departure for Lew. Never before had he been even slightly critical of another player. "I guess I'm just more critical in my old age," said the 21-year-old.

As long as Alcindor joined in the speculation, others did not hesitate to express their opinions.

Willis Reed: "I've played against Alcindor at summer camps and there's no question about it—for a big man he's well-coordinated, aggressive and pretty good on defense, too. If Wilt Chamberlain ever quits in a few years and Bill Russell slows down, Lew can be the No. 1 center in the league."

Even John Wooden had his opinion, telling one reporter that Alcindor is "the greatest player in the history of inter-collegiate basketball. He will get better and stronger each succeeding year."

Lew, meanwhile, tried to divert the pressure away from himself. "There have been some great college players who went into the pros and just didn't have it," he reminded. "And there have been some mediocre players who made good."

All of this talk was premature as the Bruins and Lew Alcindor faced the task still ahead. If winning became tedious, if there was no longer a challenge, perhaps they were shocked out of their matter-of-factness by crosstown rival, USC. It was bound to happen somewhere along the way and perhaps it was good that it happened when it did. It probably toughened them for the pressure of the NCAA championship tournament that lay ahead.

Overconfident, too casual and relaxed because they had already clinched the Pacific Eight Conference championship and the berth in the NCAA playoffs, the Bruins stumbled over Southern California late in the season. Using the stalling tactics that had, by now, become a common practice against the Alcindor menace, the Trojans sent UCLA down to a 46-44 defeat, only the second suffered by UCLA in the three-year "age of Alcindor."

"We simply had a case of the blahs," Lew explained. "But nobody was really upset about it, except that we hated to lose even that one game."

If it can happen in a regular season game to

a team like USC, the UCLA players warned themselves, it could happen in the pressure of a post-season tournament. And it almost did, in the semi-final game against Drake. Complacency set in and the Bruins found themselves ahead by one point, 83-82, with just nine seconds to go. Then Lynn Shackleford scored two foul shots and UCLA had come through its closest scare and advanced into the finals against Purdue in a position to become the first team to win three straight NCAA titles.

Ironically, UCLA had opened its season with a 94-82 victory over Purdue, but situations change. That was in Los Angeles and this was on the neutral court of Louisville's Freedom Hall before an audience of 18,699, many of whom had come in hopes of seeing the UCLA-Lew Alcindor dynasty crumble. "Nobody," Alcindor once commented, "roots for Goliath."

Purdue had improved considerably since its December meeting with UCLA. The Boilermakers had a hot-shot named Rick Mount, a skinny, 6-4 blond with uncanny accuracy on long jump shots. He was the nation's second leading scorer with a 33.8 average. And the Boilermakers had impressed by overwhelming highly rated North Carolina, 92-65, on the same night that UCLA was having its troubles with a lesser team like Drake.

It was the last game Lew Alcindor would play in college and it was the biggest, most meaningful game he had ever played. He had to admit he felt the pressure.

"It's mental. It's all up here," he said, tapping a long, bony forefinger on his head. "Everything was up in my throat all week. I could see ahead to the end, but there was apprehension and fear. Fear of losing. I don't know why, but it was there. Before the other two tournaments it didn't feel that way. This one did. But, wow, today after I came to the bench I was just yelling. Wow, I was excited. We just had to bring this thing down in front again where it belongs."

Those looking for ominous signs found them when Rick Mount scored the game's first basket, matched by Alcindor, then another by Mount on a 20-foot jumper. He looked like he was going to have one of those nights, one of those nights when everything he threw into the air went through the hoop. There's no stopping a guy when he has one of those nights, not even with an Alcindor. A guy could have a night like that and carry his team all the way to heights never before reached, all the way, Alcindor thought with a gasp, to the national championship.

But Alcindor scored again to make it 4-4 and then Kenny Heitz, the 6-4 senior with the glasses and the scholarly look, planted himself in front of Mount and stayed as close to him as Rick's next breath.

Alcindor scored nine of UCLA's first 12 points and UCLA raced to a 14-6 lead and Rick Mount was unable to shake Kenny Heitz. He went 18 minutes and 27 seconds without scoring. He took 14 shots and missed every one and finally scored on a steal and breakaway with 42 seconds left in the first half. By that time, Alcindor had scored 24 points and UCLA led, 42-31, and the pattern of the game had been firmly and emphatically established.

The pattern continued in the second half. Mount got hot, making nine of 18 shots from the field and finishing with 28 points, but UCLA and Alcindor maintained their edge. Alcindor finished with 20 rebounds and 37 points, scoring the last two points of his college career in a symbolic manner, taking a missed foul shot by sophomore John Vallely, reaching up high and casually dropping it into the basket.

Now it was almost over. All that remained was for the clock to tick off the final seconds

... of the game ... of Lew Alcindor's three-year varsity career. The "Age of Alcindor" was coming to a dramatic, sensational end and when the buzzer sounded, Lew Alcindor headed for the nearest basket, reached up and with youthful exuberance, unlaced the net and draped it around his neck for safekeeping. That would be his souvenir, his memento of a college career that was, at once, glorious and burdensome.

"The yoke is removed now," said Bill Sweek, speaking for all the UCLA players and, especially, for Alcindor. "Let them try to match us."

There were other mementoes for the UCLA giant. There was a third straight tournament Most Valuable Player trophy, the first time any player had won it three times. Jerry Lucas of Ohio State, Bob Kurland of Oklahoma A&M and Alex Groza of Kentucky had won it twice, but only Lew Alcindor had won it three times.

And there was the greatest memento of all, the unprecedented third straight national collegiate championship that belonged to all of them, but, Alcindor believed, belonged mostly to him. Not because it was he who won them, but because the burden had been on him. All the predictions that he would lead UCLA to three straight national championships had been his burden and he had done it. He had gotten a tie when the best he could get was a tie.

It was over. At last, it was over and Lew Alcindor was relieved and so were hundreds of coaches throughout the country, relieved to have passed the "Age of Alcindor." John Wooden, too, was a man relieved as he looked ahead to next year, to the start of a new age, an age without Alcindor.

"I'll be glad when I can coach to win again," he said, "instead of coaching not to lose."

The 37 points Alcindor scored in the final game of his college career gave him 2,325 points, a three-year average of 26.4 points a game. It was not a record. He did not set any records for points or rebounds, but he left his indelible stamp on the history of college basketball. He left his stamp with the three national championship trophies, for 1967, 1968 and 1969, that are housed in the trophy case in the athletic department at the University of California at Los Angeles.

The next time Lew Alcindor pulled on a uniform or laced a sneaker or scored a basket or banged into huge, muscular bodies to grab a rebound, somebody would be paying for the privilege ... somebody would be paying a lot of money for the privilege. Who it would be and where it would be still remained a mystery.

10

THE DRAFT

From all outward appearances, it was a day not unlike any other day in the workaday world of Walter Kennedy, Commissioner of the National Basketball Association. The date was March 19, 1969, a typically raw and blustery pre-spring day in the northeastern United States.

As usual, Walter Kennedy was awake shortly after seven as dawn peeked through the windows of his home in Stamford, Connecticut. He dressed in a dark blue suit, the currently fashionable dark blue shirt and striped tie, and scanned the morning newspapers over break-

134

fast. Later, on the train to New York City, he would have time to read the papers more carefully.

The hands on the clock were quickly approaching 8:30 as Walter Kennedy slipped into his overcoat and prepared to take the short walk to the New Haven Railroad's Stamford station, where he would catch the 8:47 for Grand Central. This morning he paused in a gesture that made it not unlike any other morning. He went to his den and opened a desk drawer and removed one of two John F. Kennedy half dollars that had been presented to him by the late President's brother, Senator Robert F. Kennedy. He slipped the coin into his right-hand pants pocket and headed for the station.

That coin, flipped into the air later in the day and landing either with head up or tail up, would determine which one of two NBA teams would have the negotiation rights to the most valuable piece of basketball property ever to come out of college. The team that guessed right would have the NBA's negotiation rights to Lew Alcindor and with it, the promise of instant success and the prospect of the start of a new dynasty in professional basketball. To the winner of the coin flip would go all those

135

good things. To the loser would go abject disappointment.

The two teams involved were the Milwaukee Bucks and the Phoenix Suns, both newcomers to the league when the NBA expanded in the 1968-69 season. Now, after one futile and frustrating season, they stood on the threshhold of practically guaranteed success. They earned that right by having the good sense to finish last in their respective divisions, Milwaukee in the East, Phoenix in the West.

The NBA, you understand, was not rewarding ineptness. Not exactly. If that were the case, Phoenix would have the big prize without a contest. The Suns had won only 16 out of 82 games the previous season. Milwaukee had won 11 games more. To avoid charges of collusion, the NBA had instituted the coin flip. The two last place teams, one in each division, would qualify to have their fate determined by an honest, simple, old-fashioned flip of a coin. What could be fairer?

The real loser in this case was the Detroit Pistons, an NBA team since 1948 and a team which had missed finishing last in the East (and thereby qualifying for the flip) by a mere five games.

There was no guarantee, however, that the

winner of the flip would sign Alcindor. The American Basketball Association, a new rival to the established NBA in the world of pro basketball, was making a big push to sign the UCLA star. And Alcindor was keeping an open mind about both leagues.

After UCLA had won its third consecutive NCAA title in Alcindor's last varsity game, releasing him from all collegiate ties, all the speculation came out into the open. Reporters asked him about his future.

"Pro ball is next on the agenda," he said, "but I don't even have a lawyer yet. I don't have a preference in either league right now because there are so many variables."

That night Alcindor went to see the Kentucky Colonels play the Minnesota Pipers and after the game he visited with Minnesota star, Connie Hawkins, a long-time friend from the sidewalks and playgrounds of New York City. Wherever Alcindor went that night, ABA Commissioner George Mikan was not far behind, hovering near the tall young man. And well he might. In his huge hands, Lew Alcindor held the fate of the entire league.

If he signed with the ABA, their two-year struggle for survival, their battle with the older NBA for talent and prestige, would end.

Alcindor would guarantee the ABA a national television contract and instant success

"This is my first ABA game," Alcindor told reporters. "It's not the NBA, but it's good basketball."

Alcindor was torn between two desires—the desire to play in the established NBA, which offered security and appealed to his pride by giving him the opportunity to prove himself against the best basketball players in the world; and the desire to play in New York. That would rule out the NBA. In the NBA, he would have to play either in Milwaukee or Phoenix, whichever won the flip of the coin. Commissioner Kennedy had ruled, long ago, that there would be no deals to deliver Alcindor to the New York Knickerbockers and, therefore, insure that he played in the NBA. The league was too big and too well-established to be dictated to by one player, even a Lew Alcindor.

However, in the ABA he was, coincidentally, drafted by the New York Nets, who had struggled and bathed in red ink for two years. The Nets played in Commack, Long Island, in faroff Suffolk County, Long Island. It wasn't exactly Broadway and 42nd Street, but it was the closest Alcindor was going to get to the bright lights of the Great White Way.

Alcindor added to the mystery by refusing to reveal his preference. "In the ABA," he pointed out, "I can play in New York. But the NBA is a better league. The money will figure in, too."

The money would figure very prominently. Even Alcindor's early estimate of a six-figure salary was modest. The figure was now at seven figures.

"Start at $1 million," was the word, "and go up from there."

Nobody was balking at the price. The Phoenix Suns and the Milwaukee Bucks would gladly pay it, but first they had to win the coin toss.

The 8:47 out of Stamford arrived on time at Grand Central Station, shortly before 9:30 a.m. From there, Walter Kennedy took a cab to the West Side and nine blocks downtown to his office at Two Pennsylvania Plaza, adjacent to the new Madison Square Garden. He rode the 23 floors on the elevator and was at his desk shortly before 10.

The day passed quickly. The annual NBA playoffs were about to begin and there was league business to occupy the morning for Commissioner Kennedy and a lengthy lunch uptown took care of the early afternoon. Back in his office now, he was ready for the historic coin flip.

It was 3 P.M. in New York, 2 P.M. in Milwaukee and 1 P.M. in Phoenix when the three-way conference call was made. The long-distance operator connected Commissioner Kennedy with Wes Pavalon, Chairman of the Board of the Bucks, in Milwaukee, and with Dick Bloch, President of the Suns, in Phoenix.

"Hello, Wes," said Kennedy. "I've got Dick Bloch on this line, too. Hello, Dick."

"Now," the Commissioner of the NBA said in a businesslike voice, "here's how this will work. I've got Connie Maroselli and Helenmarie Burns of my staff here as witnesses. I'm going to lay the telephone receiver on my desk. Then I will flip the coin in the air, catch it in my right hand and put it on the back of my left hand."

It had been mutually agreed that Phoenix would call first. Actually, Milwaukee yielded to Phoenix after the Bucks learned the trouble the Suns had put themselves through. Originally, in anticipation that they might call first, the Suns' general manager Jerry Colongelo flipped a coin 200 times in the air to see if there would be a preponderance of heads or tails. There wasn't. So, the Suns decided to make a promotion out of the flip. They asked fans to write in and tell them whether to call "heads" or "tails." The fans favored "heads" and "heads" it would be.

The ground rules set, Kennedy prepared to make the flip.

"OK," he said, "I'm putting the phone down."

There was silence on the other end as the Commissioner flipped the Kennedy half dollar high into the air and, in the office, the only noise was the sound of the metal coin hitting the palm of his right hand with a "slap" and then the sound of the coin being placed on the back of his left hand with another "slap."

Now Kennedy picked up the telephone and reported the news, good for one, bad for another.

"It's tails," he said, and the noise on the other end of the telephone, the Milwaukee end, was "like New Year's Eve on Broadway. Guys were yelling and screaming and slapping each other on the back."

All of a sudden, Kennedy heard somebody yell, "Ouch", and he recognized the voice of John Erickson, the Bucks' general manager.

"You won't believe what's going on here,"

141

Erickson shouted. "Pavalon just kissed me with a cigarette in his mouth."

On the other open line, there was silence and Walter Kennedy could sense the disappointment from almost 3,000 miles away. Finally, Dick Bloch broke the silence, directing his remarks to Wes Pavalon.

"I hate to say it," he mumbled, "but congratulations."

That was only half the battle. Now Wes Pavalon and the Milwaukee Bucks were faced with the big job, getting Lew Alcindor to put his name on the dotted line.

His college eligibility used up with the championship game against Purdue, Alcindor was now ready to talk to the pros. Or listen to the pros, to be exact. He met first with the NBA, represented by Commissioner Walter Kennedy and a group from Milwaukee.

On his way to the negotiations, Lew had picked up two advisers, both UCLA alumni. One was Sam Gilbert, a contractor, the other was Ralph Shapiro, a partner in a Los Angeles brokerage firm. Among the three of them, Alcindor, Gilbert and Shapiro, they had agreed they would not get involved in a long, drawn-out bidding war that would drag Lew's name

142

through the newspapers, create hard feelings to the loser and hurt his career before it started. They would get their money, to be sure, and they told both parties they would listen to one offer and one offer only; whichever was the better offer would be accepted by Lew.

Down deep, he hoped the New York Nets would come up with the best offer. "Nobody knew it at the time," Alcindor said later, "but the ABA had the inside track on me. All my life I'd dreamed of playing for the Knicks, because it's my home town and I love New York, but since the Knicks hadn't won the right to draft me, I'd have been almost as happy to play with the New York Nets in the ABA. And they had won the rights. If you give me 100 cities to play in, 99 of them would be New York."

But Alcindor had given his word, one offer and one offer only. Before the Bucks made their offer, they got some flippant advice from Detroit Pistons' coach Butch van Breda Kolff. "I don't think the NBA should negotiate with Alcindor," he quipped. "I think each team in the league should give him $100,000 and tell him to go to the beach."

The Bucks disregarded the advice and made their offer, a five-year deal. The terms were never revealed, but the best guesses said it would mean $1.4 million to Alcindor, which would make him the highest paid rookie in the history of professional basketball.

Now it was the Nets' turn and, as Lew later told it, "some strange things happened." The day after their meeting with the Bucks, Alcindor, Gilbert and Shapiro went to the Manhattan town house of Arthur Brown, the successful businessman who owned the Nets. ABA Commissioner George Mikan also attended.

The Nets' offer was also for five years. Arthur Brown put a cashier's check on the table. Reportedly, it was for $1 million. Alcindor weighed it against Milwaukee's offer. There was no choice.

"That's not as good as Milwaukee," Lew Alcindor said.

"That's as high as I can go," Arthur Brown said.

"That's it, then," Lew Alcindor said and he left with Sam Gilbert and Ralph Shapiro and returned to their hotel. They were surprised . . and Lew was disappointed. There had been rumors that the Nets' offer would come close to $2 million, that the other clubs in the ABA would add to the pot just to guarantee getting Alcindor who would be the saviour of their league. Brown declined, with thanks, any help from his colleagues.

"I have not sought any help in signing Alcindor," Brown had told an interviewer.

Back in their hotel, Alcindor and his advisers decided to call NBA Commissioner Kennedy. They gave him the good news. Lew would play with Milwaukee.

"Is this final?" Kennedy inquired. "Can I count on your word?"

"Yes," Sam Gilbert said, and Lew got on the telephone to confirm it. "You can have the papers drawn up."

That night, two representatives of the ABA contacted Gilbert in an attempt to reopen negotiations. More strange things occurred. When Gilbert said Lew had already made his decision and given his word to Commissioner Kennedy, there were more figures tossed around. The ABA threatened to sue the NBA and later it came out that the second offer had amounted to an estimated $3.25 million, including a $500,000 cash bonus, five percent ownership in the Nets, valued at $100,000, a salary of $200,000 per year for five years, an annuity of $62,500 a year for 20 years starting at age 41 and several other inducements.

It was too late. Lew Alcindor had given his word to the Milwaukee Bucks and Lew Alcindor would stick to his word.

"Our negotiator blew it," said an embittered Pat Boone, the singer of white buckskin shoes fame and an owner of the ABA's Oakland franchise.

Wes Pavalon of the Bucks was ecstatic. "It's a dream come true," said Milwaukee's Chairman of the Board. "Because of the quality of the person. He carried on his contract talks with the greatest trust and integrity I've been a part of."

On Saturday, October 18, 1969, the Milwaukee Bucks opened their season at home against the Detroit Pistons and the starting center for the Bucks was No. 33, Lew Alcindor. Later that night, the Bucks had a dinner in Milwaukee's Pfister Hotel. In attendance was Walter Kennedy, Commissioner of the National Basketball Association. When he was called upon to speak, Kennedy made his remarks brief, then closed by presenting Wes Pavalon with the John F. Kennedy half dollar he had used on the afternoon of March 19, 1969, to determine which NBA team would win the negotiation rights to Lew Alcindor.

Pavalon gratefully accepted the coin and

threw his arms around Kennedy in a warm embrace. Only those closest to him on the dais could see the tears of joy in Wes Pavalon's eyes.

11
ADVICE

In exchange for his signature on a contract, Lew Alcindor had 1,400,000 of the Milwaukee Bucks' bucks. He figured it was a fair exchange. He also had, at absolutely no charge, plenty of advice. It came from all over the country, from people in all walks of life, corroborating the belief that Lew would be the most talked about rookie to come into the National Basketball Association in many years.

Most of the advice came from the NBA's big men, the people who would be playing head-to-head against Alcindor. And not all of it was advice. Some of it was a warning, with the general tone that if Alcindor thinks he will do in the pro league what he did in college, he's in for a surprise.

Alcindor was the new kid on the block and there were magazine articles describing, in gory detail, how the big, strong, rugged brutes of the NBA would break him in half. It set up a continuing debate, a pro and con, back-and-forth series of arguments on the relative merits of Lew Alcindor and how he would do in the pro league. All of which, quite naturally, were greatly enjoyed by owners and general managers around the league.

"Lew is coming in with a big name, a very large name," said Elvin Hayes, Alcindor's old protagonist from the University of Houston, now a star with the San Diego Rockets. "A lot of players will be keying on him. They'll want to say they stopped Lew Alcindor, that they beat him, and he's going to have a ton of pressure on him. Whenever he goes into a town people will come out just to see him, to see what he can do and their eyes will be focused right on him. I really feel sorry for the guy. There are so many people just sitting around waiting, looking for so much, expecting so much, and hoping he falls on his face."

Said Atlanta coach, Richie Guerin: "I'm sure

he'll be a big star, but he won't have a picnic out there every night. Nearly every club in the league has an outstanding center now and Alcindor will have to learn how to use his skills against each individual—men like Wilt Chamberlain and Nate Thurmond."

Lew Alcindor was ready for them. He didn't expect life in the NBA to be a family picnic on a Sunday afternoon. He expected it to be rough. He also expected it to be a two-way street.

"I might make it rough for them," he warned. "If they're aiming for me, I've got to be aiming for them, too. I'm not going into this thing with blinders on. I think I know what to expect."

In reply to those who said he would have to add a few pounds to the 240 he was carrying on his gigantic frame, Alcindor said: "If I put on more weight, I won't be able to move as well. I wouldn't be able to rely on my quickness and know-how. I expect to be stronger, but not necessarily heavier."

To clear up one misconception, the Knicks' Willis Reed observed: "I don't think anybody's out to get him. Naturally, you don't want to be outplayed by anybody, particularly a rookie. He's going to find out this league is tougher than college. There's more pushing, more shoving, more hitting. All I know about Lew is that he's tall and as far as I'm concerned, he's just one more guy I have to worry about. I just have to go out and do the job. It means I have to work a little harder to make a living. He's a great player. He's got height and skill and he's been a winner. I can't see how he can miss being a star in our league."

There were others who shared the Knick star's evaluation of Alcindor. Lew's college coach, John Wooden, for instance.

"I think Lewis will be like the player he was in college," Wooden predicted. "Although, it's difficult to dominate the pro game, there is no question that Lewis is going to be an instantaneous success in the pros."

It was at a New York restaurant, at a luncheon honoring him as the Most Valuable Player in the 1969 NBA playoffs, that Jerry West of the Los Angeles Lakers got to his feet and said if he were starting a team, the first player he would pick would be Lew Alcindor.

Naturally, someone said, what he meant was that he would want Lew for his youth, his potential and because he had such a great career ahead of him.

"No," Jerry West replied: "I mean for one

year. I mean right now. I've seen him play many times and I believe he's the best big man in the game already."

It was, considering that Lew had only just graduated from college a few days before, a startling opinion and an overwhelming endorsement for Alcindor. While others heaped praise on him and made predictions of great things for him, Alcindor tempered all the wild enthusiasm with a note of caution.

"I've heard some people say that I'm going to tear the game apart, ruin pro basketball with my height and my moves," he repeated. "Nobody who knows pro basketball can take a statement like that seriously. I'm going to be a rookie and I'm going to have a lot to learn like every rookie in the league, and if I take the NBA apart, then that must have been an optical illusion I was watching when I saw all those NBA games and watched men like Wilt Chamberlain and Jerry West and Elvin Hayes do their tricks out there. Nobody is going to take those cats apart."

He had not yet played his first game in the NBA, yet the predictions were flying all around him. A lesser young man than Alcindor would not have been able to keep his perspective. "It doesn't affect me," Lew said. "I believe when

152

you know yourself, realize your own identity and what is expected of you, then it's really no bother at all. This is what I must get used to."

Inevitably, comparisons were made between Lew and Wilt Chamberlain, the standard for big men in the NBA. He was as tall as Lew (although many insisted Alcindor had at least an inch on the 7-2 Wilt), he was much stronger than Lew and he had come into the league a decade earlier with as much ballyhoo as Alcindor was receiving. But Chamberlain had already produced. He was the greatest scorer in NBA history and still going strong. Playing against Chamberlain, a confrontation all basketball fans anticipated with great glee, was something Lew neither looked forward to nor feared. "I don't think anybody looks forward to it [playing against Wilt]," he said. "It's a challenge. If I can do it and be successful, that's a feather in my cap."

The controversy of Lew Alcindor raged, fanned by the fire started by his old college rival, Elvin Hayes. The Big E was killing Alcindor with kindness. "I'm one of those who hopes he does well because I think he's good for the league," Elvin would say. Then, before his words had settled, he would add, "He's good, but he's also lucky. He got his start in New

York, where the big writers are, and by the time he was a senior in high school they were saying he was good enough for the pros. Then he played college ball in Los Angeles, where they make a big production out of everything. There have been other high school players in Lew's class [no names, please, Elvin], but you never heard of them. If Lew just finishes out the season, he will be rookie of the year in the NBA, and he will make the all-star team over somebody who deserves it more."

No, the Big E was not finished talking. Not yet. "First, you ask yourself how Lew will adjust to playing with a bad team. Lew was a great player at UCLA, but he wasn't by himself. He has never been a graceful loser. And now he will get plenty of chances."

There were, however, some people who were not so sure. Among them were Jerry West and Bill Sharman, former Boston Celtic star and coach of the Los Angeles Stars in the ABA, who pointed out several facts in Alcindor's favor.

"Offensively," said Sharman, "Lew should be even more productive as a pro than he was as a collegian. In college, he had to fight all sorts of gimmick defenses and stalls and double and triple-teaming. But in the pros, he'll have more freedom on offense. And he can dunk, too."

This freedom, Jerry West added, would also be provided by the NBA's 24-second clock, which eliminated the stall. "With the clock," the Laker star said, "he'll have a better chance to play his game. In college he was restricted a great deal. When he plays in our league, you're going to see Lew do things he's never done before. The hard part will be getting psychologically prepared for an 82-game schedule. But I think he has an unlimited future in this league. He wouldn't even have to score points and he'd still be a valuable player."

Yet, somebody would always bring up Lew's physique and the problems he would have in the rugged NBA. Somebody like Elvin Hayes.

"The big thing for Lew will be how he reacts to the physical punishment," Elvin said. "This is a muscle game they play up here. If he can take the pushing and the shoving and jabbing, if he can keep from losing his temper, he'll be okay. But if he says, 'You can't get away with that, I'll show you,' then he's in trouble. The big boys, they can get away with it. In pro basketball, the veteran is it. A rookie is nothing. You don't talk back. You don't get smart.

You don't make them mad. You don't cause trouble. Lew has got to learn this."

Lew heard all the things they were saying about him, read all the criticisms, but characteristically, he remained mute. He refused to answer words with words. He would answer with actions when the right time came. It came sooner than he thought it would.

It came in June, in a pickup game in Los Angeles. Alcindor found himself playing against Dennis Grey, a rugged 6-8 with a reputation for rough play. Actually, Alcindor *felt* himself playing against Dennis Grey. For a long time he took it, the slap-slap, the digging, the slamming of bodies, the elbows, knees, hips . . . and the taunts.

"If you can't take it in a pickup game," Dennis Grey chided, "you'll be killed by Chamberlain and Russell."

Alcindor took it for as long as he could and then he could take it no more. The time had come. After one particularly bruising scuffle during which Dennis Grey had used his best playground weapon—a well-placed elbow—Lew turned around and landed a right to Dennis Grey's jaw. It took a team of doctors two hours to set the jaw, which had been broken in two places. Lew Alcindor had served warning on the big men of the NBA.

Now the words changed. "Playground basketball is rough," said Willis Reed. "It's almost like Viet Nam. Evidently he felt like the guy needed to be hit, so he hit him."

"If you ask me what I think," said Elvin Hayes, "I'll tell you that he'll make it. He's stronger than he looks. A lot of guys in our league, they are in for a surprise. They're going to say, 'Oh, he looks so frail, he looks so weak.' And they're going to wake up with welts on their head."

Shortly after the Dennis Grey incident, Alcindor went to Milwaukee to officially sign his contract for the benefit of the press, radio and television. The signing was greeted with all the pomp and ceremony that might be expected for such a momentous event and the most pleased person at the signing was Larry Costello, whose good fortune it would be to coach the man many consider the pro game's next superstar.

"We'll be able to play a different game entirely with Lew," Costello told the press. "Last year we worked out of the corners most of the time. Now we'll drive right through the middle. Playing with Lew, you can just throw the ball in the air and you won't have to worry. He'll get it. Lew is the type of player who intimidates anybody who comes into the middle. He blocks so many shots that he forces the opposition to change its offense. He's taller than Wilt Chamberlain. And quicker too.

"Lew has the talent to shoot from the outside, but since he's 7-4, I'd rather have him under the basket."

The crowd of reporters buzzed as Costello's words sank in . . . "since he's 7-4 . . ."

Had Costello inadvertently let something out of the bag? Or was it a conscious slip, one that would give Alcindor a psychological edge over his opponents?

"We just measured him," said Jim Foley, the Bucks' director of publicity, "and from his bare feet to the top of his head he was exactly 7-1⅝."

What Foley failed to mention was that wearing his hair in a modified version of the modern Afro style, wearing two pairs of thick woolen socks and the thick-soled basketball shoes, Lew stood close to 7-6. And when he raised his long, slender arms or jumped, he gave the impression of a New York skyscraper that moves.

To say that Lew Alcindor is tall is like saying

Raquel Welch is a girl, Frank Sinatra has a voice, Arthur Rubinstein is a piano player.

Interviewed on television, Alcindor was humble. He would not predict instant success as a pro, although within him there still abided confidence and a desire to succeed.

"Everyone realizes that this is the NBA and people recognize this is the best competition, the toughest league and the toughest division of the league," he said. "So I don't think too many people will be disappointed if we don't win every game. It's not a question of how we're going to play, but how I'm going to play for coach Costello. He knows a lot more about basketball than I do."

Lew agreed that the pro game, with a 24-second clock, a ban on zone defenses and the freedom to dunk would help him make full use of his individual skills. He noted that his best scoring season in college was his sophomore year, before the "Alcindor Rule" banned the dunk shot. "It will be good to be able to dunk the ball again," he said in a masterpiece of understatement.

During that summer before Alcindor's rookie season, Bill Russell announced his retirement and Zelmo Beaty, Atlanta's skilled center, jumped from the NBA to the ABA, thereby removing two great obstacles from Alcindor's path. Russell, always a prideful man, resented suggestions that he was getting out because Alcindor was coming into the League to threaten his role as the NBA's dominant defensive player.

Pete Newell, general manager of the San Diego Rockets, noted that Alcindor "comes as close defensively to Russell as anyone has ever been. Particularly in instincts and reactions. He is going to cause a lot of teams to adjust their offense. Whether it's rebounding or blocking shots, he's going to get a lot of balls that Russell wouldn't get."

Afraid of Alcindor? Ridiculous, said Russell. "I've never been afraid of anybody before. As great as Alcindor is, he won't have the impact on the league that Chamberlain had because Wilt was the first player of his size to come into our league and produce. I think Alcindor is going to be the greatest center who ever played the game. He's had an advantage. Since he's been in tenth grade, he had the advantage of being able to watch guys like me and Wilt and learn from us."

Elvin Hayes seized upon Russell's retirement and the accompanying controversy to get in a few more shots at his favorite whipping boy.

"Nobody will be able to psych Lew," he said, "although I wish Bill Russell was still around. It would be fun to see what Russell would do with him. He was the master."

Then Hayes set up a hypothetical comparison. "I'm Russell, see, and he's Wilt. I'm 6-9½ just like Russell, and Lew is about the same height as Wilt. You got to have new names, and we got this thing between us. Nothing personal. But whenever people put us together, they just want to see us crash and go after it."

Elvin's message was lost on no one. He did not have to point out that Russell always had it over Chamberlain, like a jinx, despite the difference in height. There was no mistaking the suggestion that Alcindor would be to Hayes what Chamberlain was to Russell.

It was getting close to the time when Lew Alcindor would have to put it on the line. The people of Milwaukee could hardly wait. All the controversy, all the opinion, all the speculation had served their purpose, filling Milwaukee's two newspapers, the *Journal* and the *Sentinel*, through a long and dull summer.

In July, the citizens of Milwaukee got a hint of what life would be like with Lew Alcindor. So did the Bucks' players and management. Everybody liked what they saw. In their first year, the Bucks had an average attendance of 6,000 per game at home. Charging a $2 admission for an intra-squad game in July, the Bucks drew 10,482 fans and collected their first dividend on a $1.4 million insurance policy.

There were other dividends. Alcindor scored 35 points, hitting on 15 of 27 shots from the floor, grabbed 23 rebounds, led his white-jerseyed team over a Milwaukee green-jerseyed team, 125-118, and won the respect of his new fans and his new teammates.

"He's everything we've heard about him and maybe more," said Flynn Robinson. "He moves better and handles the ball better than any big man in our league. He has a fine shooting touch and, of course, he can rebound. And on defense, well, he does have it all there too."

Rich Niemann, the seven-footer who had to play opposite Alcindor, heaped praise on the big guy. "Lew's unbelievably graceful. He makes it look so easy. He doesn't appear to be strong physically, but he is strong. He holds his own."

"I haven't seen any center in pro basketball dribble like that, the way he changes hands and comes at you aggressively," raved coach Larry Costello.

The Bucks were ecstatic. They had taken it

on the chin from the rest of the NBA the previous season and they had some scores to settle. Things, they figured, were going to be different with Lew Alcindor on their side.

12

THE PRO

All the talk could not help Lew Alcindor now. All the advice, all the speculation, all the opinion, all the warnings, all the suggestions had come and gone. Now there was only Lew Alcindor, alone, and it was time for him to put it on the line. Words could not help him. Only deeds would count now.

His debut came on Saturday, October, 18, 1969, against the Detroit Pistons and before a capacity crowd in Milwaukee and a national television audience. His parents had come in from New York to be there and the American Broadcasting Company had requested the game be moved to the afternoon so that it could be part of the network's "Wide World of Sport" show.

What would you expect of a 22-year-old rookie playing his first game in the National Basketball Association? Would you expect him to score 14 points in the first period and to finish the game with 29 points on 12 of 27 from the floor? Would you expect him to grab 12 rebounds, block three shots—also two others which were ruled goaltending? Would you expect him to play all 48 minutes, contribute six assists and three steals and handle the ball like a six-footer? Do you think that's too much to expect of a 22-year-old rookie playing his first game in the National Basketball Association? Well, that's what 22-year-old Lew Alcindor did, in a game won by the Bucks, 119-110.

Lew Alcindor did something else after the game, something that certified him as a truly remarkable rookie with a marvelous future. What Lew Alcindor did was express disappointment with his debut.

"I didn't care too much for my play," he analyzed. "I made a lot of mistakes. I took some bad shots for one thing. The rest of my game was a little help, but I know I can do better."

Alcindor's opinion of himself was a minority one. Everyone else was greatly impressed. Such as former NBA star, Jack Twyman, now an ABC commentator.

"This could be the start of something big in Milwaukee," Twyman guessed. "Alcindor plays like [Bill] Russell. And he's a better shooter. But beyond his shooting, I was impressed with the way he made the team move. His ability to hit the open man is amazing. He's a complete ballplayer and a very unselfish ballplayer. His teammates know that if they get open, they'll get the ball."

"He ought to be able to see the open man," snorted Detroit coach, Bill van Breda Kolff. "He's looking down on everybody."

In Alcindor's second game, the Bucks easily defeated the Seattle SuperSonics and they moved to San Diego for the third game of the season, a game that had been anticipated for weeks. The Milwaukee Bucks vs. the San Diego Rockets; Lew Alcindor vs. Elvin Hayes; their first meeting since the semi-finals of the 1968 NCAA tournament; their first meeting as pros; their first meeting since Hayes' widely-circulated printed opinions of Alcindor.

"First, you ask yourself how Lew will adjust to playing with a bad team."

166

In their first meeting, Alcindor's Milwaukee team defeated Hayes' San Diego team, 115-102.

"The big thing for Lew will be how he reacts to the physical punishment. This is a muscle game they play up here."

In their first meeting, Alcindor scored 36 points to Hayes' 21 and outrebounded Elvin, 19-15.

"He has never been a graceful loser."

In their first meeting, Alcindor made 15 of 26 shots from the floor, all from within six feet of the basket; Hayes, forced to go outside, made only nine of 31 and sat out most of the third period. "I had a headache," Elvin said. The headache was wearing No. 33 on a Milwaukee Bucks' uniform.

Alcindor's Bucks beat Hayes' Rockets all six times they met during the season and in five of those games, Lew outscored his old college rival. It was a fairly conclusive decision.

"Lew is a superior player in every respect," said his coach, Larry Costello. "Hayes played him hard, but there's no question in my mind who's the greatest."

Two nights later, the Bucks met the Los Angeles Lakers and Lew Alcindor played opposite Wilt Chamberlain for the first time. It was the first confrontation of the two biggest men in pro basketball and it attracted 17,487 to the Forum for the return of Lew Alcindor to Los Angeles. In the first half, the advantage was Alcindor's. He outscored Chamberlain, 12-7, and helped the Bucks to a 60-54 lead.

Chamberlain came back strong in the second half. Responding to the challenge of the rookie, Wilt scored 18 points in the second half. He outscored Lew, 25-23, outshot him (nine of 14 to nine of 21 for Alcindor) and outrebounded him, 25-20, as Los Angeles sent Alcindor and the Bucks down to their first defeat, 123-112.

Late in the game, Milwaukee had scored eight straight points to come within two points of tying the score. With a chance to tie, Alcindor went for the hoop, but Chamberlain put out his greatest effort, blocked the shot and the Lakers went on to an 8-0 streak to break the game apart.

"This was the first time I ever played against Wilt for real," Alcindor said. "I learned a few things. I was just a skinny kid out there and he's the master."

Chamberlain was a gracious winner. "Lew is good," he commented, "no doubt about it. One time I had him stopped and he just switched to his left hand and went around me. I thought he was more physical than I was. I'm not saying I was dissatisfied. I never am. I didn't think my game was smooth, although Lew probably had something to do with that."

Someone mentioned that Wilt seemed to try harder in the second half, as if to keep from being outplayed by a mere rookie. "No, I didn't try harder against him," he replied. "Not consciously at least. I tried to stay relaxed and keep the game in its proper perspective, as the fifth game out of 82. This is actually preseason for the playoffs. Milwaukee is going to be a contender this year, so it was a matter of experimenting for later on."

Actually, Alcindor's first meeting against Chamberlain was not a disaster for the rookie. Chamberlain had had the upper hand, no argument there. But it was not a conclusive triumph for the veteran Wilt, the incumbent giant of the NBA. Alcindor would make a better showing in their future meetings, meetings that were looked forward to with great anticipation. But they were meetings that never came off. A short time later, Chamberlain injured his right knee, requiring an operation. He sat out most of the season and he and Alcindor never appeared on the same court again that season. When Chamberlain did return, the Lakers and Bucks had completed their season's series, Los Angeles losing three of the five games they played without Wilt.

Lew Alcindor was a man in a showcase and in only a matter of weeks, he had made a tremendous impact on pro basketball. They were still talking about him, but now they were not talking about what he would accomplish, they were talking about what he had already accomplished. And he had accomplished plenty. His name was on the top of the NBA charts in scoring and rebounding; he had the Bucks challenging the New York Knicks for the top spot in the eastern division; and he was helping to fill arenas all over the league. Milwaukee's attendance was up more than 50 percent, to the everlasting gratitude of Alcindor's bosses.

John Erickson, Bucks' general manager for instance: "Last year nobody knew we were in town when we played on the road. We'd sneak in, sneak out, and in the meantime, play a game. The exposure this year has been almost unbelievable. Batteries of people follow the team around, and the amount of print and publicity we've received in Milwaukee is far more than last season."

There was no sneaking in and sneaking out of towns with Alcindor, or maybe you never tried to hide a 7-2 basketball player. Newsmen and photographers and fans greeted the Bucks at airports, in hotels, in restaurants, on city streets.

But Alcindor was not simply a curio, as he had been in college. The pros had seen other seven-footers. They were not impressed by size alone. They were impressed by the man's skills, his poise, his grace, his knowledge. In the most demanding game and to the most critical audience—his colleagues—Lew Alcindor was winning acclaim and respect after only six weeks in the league.

No other rookie had broken into the league with such acclaim, not even Wilt Chamberlain. Perhaps it was because in the decade since Chamberlain came into the league, the game was getting much more exposure and the quality of play had improved tremendously. Alcindor was able to break in and excel in a league that was far superior to the one Chamberlain had entered.

Guy Rodgers, the Bucks' remarkable veteran guard, became the resident authority on the Chamberlain vs. Alcindor comparison. Guy, a knowledgeable basketball man and a person expresses himself well, had played with Chamberlain when Wilt was a rookie, and was playing with Lew in his rookie year.

"The best way to be honest and fair," Rodgers stressed, "is to compare them at the same stage. Wilt was a lot stronger, but not as versatile. Lew is the most agile big man I ever saw and the fastest [in pre-season training, the Bucks ran a 300-yard time trial and Alcindor beat them all, covering the distance in 38.9 seconds]. He moves around. You pass him the ball and he can put it down [dribble], move on the man guarding him and score. And he's great at the lead pass to start a fast break.

"Wilt broke all the scoring records, the 100-point game, for instance. I was convinced they wouldn't be touched. I'm now convinced that one day, if Lew gets hot, he can do it, although he's not the type to hog the ball. He has a tremendous knowledge of the game. Lots of people look on him as a 22-year-old but he's quite a ballplayer and a hell of a man."

If you really want to find out how good a ballplayer is, you do not go to his teammates; you go to his opponents, the people who play against him. If a man can pass the critical judgment of his enemies, he has passed the severest test.

Willis Reed, New York Knicks: "Nobody of his age has comparable talents. One day the guy is going to wake up and find out how really

172

good he is. I hope he doesn't. Given time, he'll be the best center in the league."

Bob Cousy, coach, Cincinnati Royals: "He's the only man I've seen with the possibility of combining Bill Russell's mental concentration with Wilt Chamberlain's physical dominance."

Tom Heinsohn, coach, Boston Celtics: "He's of superstar status right now [after 15 games]. He has the best aspects of Russell and Chamberlain in one ballplayer. Wilt is much stronger and he overpowers you to score. But Lew is still going to be a great scorer because I think he can shoot better than Chamberlain. On defense, potentially, he can do the things that Russell could do."

John Kerr, coach, Phoenix Suns: "He's going to put a lot of people into retirement."

Walt Hazzard, Atlanta Hawks: "This league hasn't seen a big fellow like large Lew. He doesn't shoot a layup, he shoots a laydown.

Tom Van Arsdale, Cincinnati Royals: mountain under that basket. Nobody's go stop him unless some guy 7-10 comes alon.

Nobody was going to stop him, but the tried. Oh, how they tried. They tested him early. They tried to provoke him. They tried to get him to blow his cool. They wanted to see if he could stand up to it. They found out he could and they found out the hard way, with elbows and fists in vicious retaliation. It was a rough few weeks for Alcindor, but it was a necessary few weeks. He could not back off. He had to establish himself right from the beginning. He had to put a stop to the rough stuff right here, right now, or be prepared to endure it for the rest of his career.

Sometimes he let it get out of hand. Sometimes he did things that he would have liked not to do. Often he was wrong. But he accomplished what he set out to accomplish.

In Philadelphia on October 31, Darrall Imhoff, the 76ers huge center, shoved him and Lew spun around, elbow first, and hit Imhoff and Darrall plummeted to the floor. The Philadelphia fans, those loud and intense and ardent followers, rained down a chorus of boos on Alcindor, the transgressor. And Lew held up the index and middle finger of his right hand, the famous Winston Churchill "V for Victory" of another generation, but the "peace" sign of this generation.

More boos. And Lew thrust his right hand, fist clenched, toward the roof in the familiar symbol of black power. More boos. But Alcindor had done what had to be done. There would be no more trouble with Darrall Imhoff for the rest of the year.

In New York the following night, Alcindor almost made a terrible mistake. He almost tangled with Willis Reed. The Knicks' captain had gone up powerfully to grab a rebound, came down and fired the ball down court. As he did, Willis felt somebody hit him from behind and he wheeled around and fired a stray elbow and menacingly raised his fists at his assailant. It was Alcindor.

"I was getting pushed and I guess I hit him and he got mad," Alcindor said later. "I didn't hit him on purpose, then he hit me. I told him it wasn't on purpose."

The two giants strolled side by side down the court.

"Forget it," said Reed. "It's over."

Alcindor was happy to forget it.

Two nights later in Milwaukee, also against the Knicks, Alcindor found himself alone underneath for a layup. Suddenly, there was Mike Riordan, a foot shorter than Lew, wrapping his arms around the big guy to keep him from shooting. A harmless, common foul.

Alcindor spun around, elbow flying, and he caught Riordan in the right cheek.

"What I said to him was unprintable," Riordan later reported.

"It was a legitimate foul," said coach Red Holzman. "He didn't try to hurt anybody and he caught an elbow for no reason."

"I didn't like the way he hit me and I hit him back," Alcindor explained. "They blew the foul and I walked away."

In the Knicks' dressing room, Riordan was explaining the incident to teammate Walt Frazier. "I was just trying to give a foul," Mike said.

"Wilt never throws elbows," Frazier replied.

"Chamberlain probably doesn't even feel a fly like me," said Riordan. "I was just looking to hold his shooting arm. Then I saw Willis coming down at him and I knew everything was all right. Willis takes care of my life's work."

It was a rough weekend for Alcindor, three altercations in four nights. And he was getting the worst of it, a reputation as a crybaby. It would have to stop. Alcindor was willing. But the others wouldn't let him.

Playing against San Diego in the Houston Astrodome later in the season, there was more unpleasantness. Elvin Hayes had fouled out and was replaced by John Block, a rough customer standing 6-10. After one scuffle under the basket, there were words exchanged between Alcindor and Block, some very unpleasant words according to Block.

"I got hit and told him to stop pushing," Alcindor explained. "I blew off some hot air. That's all there was to it. It was nothing."

"I was playing rough under the basket," said Block. "But I thought that was the way the game was supposed to be played."

In Seattle, there was a fracas with two SuperSonics, John Tresvant and Bob Rule.

"Tresvant hit me a couple of times," Lew said.

"And Rule got a finger in my eye. Man, I went for Rule. And I spit. And a kid, some bad-mouthed teenager, I gave him a shove. And I want to stand for something positive and I managed to have everyone in the whole arena dislike me. I was a protagonist. When I went for Rule there was murder in my heart."

He had said, back when he was a sophomore in college, that he wanted to "try to represent something positive for the people in the community because you know how kids idolize people and it's not good that these idols are something you wouldn't want your kid to be. So, if you take the responsibility on yourself to give him something to look up to, maybe that's one way to encourage them. I just want people to respect me. If you get respect and you earn it, you're doing yourself justice."

When he went after Bob Rule, Alcindor probably thought about his words and that turned him off. Was this the way to get respect? Well, there was another respect he had to get . . . respect on the court. He couldn't allow himself to be pushed around. Once he had established that, things would be much simpler. He had to establish that. He had to get that respect. And, in so doing, he knew he would have to hurt some innocent people and antagonize a whole lot of people. But it was done and things would be better from then on. So, too, would Lew Alcindor.

There was more unpleasantness of a different nature that first year, unpleasantness with the press. He had stepped off a plane in Detroit after a long, exhausting trip and he had been directed to an impromptu press conference, arranged without his knowledge. Tired, annoyed and feeling slightly put upon, Lew was hardly an entertaining or willing subject. His answers were monosyllablic, very unsatisfactory, and he had been harshly criticized by a Detroit columnist.

"Every writer in every city expects me to tell him something I haven't told the others," he said. "I realize it's their job, but I guess I still make some of them angry."

His coach, Larry Costello, came hurriedly to his star center's defense. "You have to realize he was sheltered from all this in high school and college," he pointed out. "Now he's in the limelight everywhere he goes and he has to handle it himself. He has a bigger adjustment to make than ordinary rookies. He's a good kid, but maybe not as colorful to the press as Chamberlain. He's been pushed around and everybody is watching him—fans, players, officials."

There was a tendency to forget that Wilt had been brooding and sullen as a youngster. Only in recent years did he change and become friendly and outgoing. Alcindor had a long way to go and a whole lot to learn.

In New York, he told columnist Milt Gross: "Sometimes I feel I was here before Buddha. Sometimes I feel I'm three years old. It all depends. I have it inside and maybe I'll catch it on the other side."

There were other problems. The fans and the press looked at him trailing nine players down court and they deduced that he was lazy. They looked at his expressionless face and they deduced that he was unconcerned. They accused him of being lazy. It was an unfair and unknowing judgment.

"I have a hyperactive mind," he once said. "I have to clear my mind to play basketball. I can't have it all cluttered. That's why I look relaxed, but I'm not relaxed. I'm all worked up, man, deep down inside."

"He does things so easy that maybe they think he's loafing," Costello commented. "He has to play a lot of minutes for us. He has to get a breather sometime and the time to get it is when we're in a fast break. When we have to set up to go for the basket, we want him in the pivot."

Perhaps it is doing Alcindor a disservice to bring up all the unpleasantness of his first year as a professional—the violence on the court, the loss of temper, the disagreements with the press, the criticism of the fans. They are merely isolated incidents in an 82-game season, a season that began with an exhibition game in July and extended until the following May.

There were so many other incidents in that year, so many good things to mention. Yet, the unpleasant things are the true measure of Lew Alcindor, his importance and his impact on the world of professional basketball. For him, that rookie year was like life in a goldfish bowl. But that is the price one must pay for success. The mediocre player can do things and they are overlooked. The great ones do the same things and they are magnified. Lew Alcindor was learning what it is like to be a star.

And make no mistake, Lew Alcindor was a star in his first year.

Elvin Hayes suggested Alcindor would make the all-star team on his name. He made the all-star team, but he made it not on his name, he made it on his merit.

Others suggested that he would be too frail, too weak for the murderous 82-game NBA schedule, but he averaged 43 minutes a game.

Some said he would not be able to do the things in the pro league that he had done in college, but he scored at the rate of 28.8 points a game, finishing second in the league to the Lakers' Jerry West.

Some said he would find the rugged rebounders of the NBA too strong for him to cope with, but he picked off an average of 14.5 rebounds a game, which placed him third behind Hayes and Baltimore's Wes Unseld.

He led all the NBA's centers with 337 assists.

He was an almost unanimous choice as Rookie of the Year, polling 145 out of a possible 146 votes cast by NBA players.

He finished third to Willis Reed of the Knicks and Jerry West of the Lakers in the balloting for the league's Most Valuable Player award, collecting 30 first place votes, and West, disappointed at not winning the prize, said if he didn't win it, he thought Alcindor should have.

He finished second, by 19/1000th of a vote behind Reed in the voting for the center spot on the all-league team.

He finished second to Reed on the all-defense team.

But most important, he led the second-year Bucks to a second place finish in the NBA East, just four games behind the Knicks and six games ahead of the defending champion Baltimore Bullets. With Alcindor in the lineup, the Bucks won 56 of 82 games, more than doubling their victory output of the previous year.

It put the Bucks into the division playoffs, a young and rapidly-improving team. The Bucks were coming and coming fast and the more established Knicks were taking uneasy glances over their shoulder in the final weeks of the season.

Would the Bucks continue to improve during

the playoffs? Their chances rested heavily on the man in the middle, the tall center who had not yet celebrated his twenty-third birthday and who wore the number 33 on his uniform.

Their chances rested on Lew Alcindor.

13

THE PLAYOFFS

The word came out of Philadelphia and spread across the country. Lew Alcindor and the young Milwaukee Bucks were on the rampage. Behind their sensational rookie center, the young Bucks had demolished the veteran Philadelphia 76ers, four games to one, in the first round of the NBA East playoffs. And they had done it with ease.

In the final game, Lew Alcindor had scored 46 points, bringing his five-game playoff scoring total to 181 points, an average of 36.2 per game. In Game No. 3, he played only 34 minutes, but scored 33 points and grabbed 17 rebounds as the Bucks beat the 76ers in Philadelphia, 156-120.

The news was a bombshell in Baltimore and New York, where the Bullets and Knicks were engaged in a fierce struggle to determine which team would move on to face the Bucks for the championship of the east. To the beaten and convinced members of the Philadelphia 76ers, it was a moot point. They agreed, to a man, that nothing could stop the Bucks now.

"Devastating." was the word 76er star Billy Cunningham used to describe Alcindor. "He's made the greatest improvement I've ever seen by a player in one season."

Coach Jack Ramsay agreed. "If I had to make a pick as to the team that will win the NBA title, it's got to be Milwaukee because of Alcindor. Put him on any team and they will win the title. He's the greatest scorer in pro basketball."

Meanwhile, the Knicks struggled through and defeated the Bullets in seven hard-fought games. It left them physically fatigued and emotionally drained as they prepared to meet the well-rested Bucks.

It was a dream match, Lew Alcindor playing in his home town against the team for whom he had rooted since he was a little boy; the

185

young and improving Bucks playing against a smart, veteran team, one that had finished with the best record in the NBA and had been acclaimed, by some, as the most exciting professional team ever put together.

There were others, though, who seriously questioned if the Knicks could hold off the oncoming Bucks and Lew Alcindor, who seemed to improve noticeably with each game they played. In six regular season games with the Knicks, the Bucks won only two. Significantly, they dropped the first four, all played before the first of the year, then won the last two. It was considered evidence of the improvement of the Bucks.

Many had reduced this series to a simple equation: Lew Alcindor vs. Willis Reed, the winner to go on to become world champion. It was as if they were Aaron Burr and Alexander Hamilton, with all that the historical analogy implied.

There was no question that Alcindor and Reed were the central figures in the series, the vital ingredients for their teams. Milwaukee's chances rested almost totally on Alcindor. New York could win without a big offensive effort from Reed, but they needed Willis to do the job on defense against Alcindor and keep the rookie's production within reason. In their six meetings, Reed had outplayed Alcindor just once. He was outscored by the Buck, 171-101, and outrebounded, 98-54, for the six games.

"I don't think this is a duel," Willis Reed said. "People are trying to create that. It's not that kind of thing. If it comes down to Alcindor getting 50 and we win, I'll take that."

Alcindor agreed. All the talk of a Reed-Alcindor duel, he said, was an "oversimplification. I'm important to my team and he's important to his, but there are other guys out there and what they do will determine what happens in this series. Suppose I went out and outplayed him and we lost . . . then I'm not doing my job. And if I don't outplay him, that doesn't matter if we win."

It was Saturday afternoon, April 11, 1970, less than an hour before he would go out on the Madison Square Garden floor for the first game of the series with the Knicks. He had walked into the Bucks' dressing room and, like an alarm clock's early morning buzz, his presence triggered action. Three reporters, who had been waiting there, sprang to their feet and drifted over to the corner where he was sitting, slowly removing his street clothes, methodically preparing for the battle that lay ahead.

Earlier, the talk had been about Alcindor.

"No one man can stop him," said John McGlocklin, the Bucks' guard. "Only God can stop his hook shot."

This is the confidence he had instilled in a team that was floating around in the depths of pro basketball before he arrived. Now they looked to him to propel them to heights they never dreamed possible.

"Hey," shouted the veteran Guy Rodgers to the small circle of reporters. "Leave my man alone. He's got to get himself together for this big game."

"You mean he's uptight about this game?" a reporter asked and Guy Rodgers laughed.

"I saw him play in high school," the veteran said, "and he was more uptight then than he is now."

Lew Alcindor bent his huge body and calmly tied the shoelace on his sneaker. In a few minutes, he would be on the Garden floor and he would throw in a hook shot with no more emotion than he showed tying his shoelace. And each time he threw in a hook shot, he would bring the Milwaukee Bucks closer to the realization of their impossible dream.

Lining up alongside Willis Reed for the opening tap, the disparity in size was alarming.

And for the first few minutes of the game, the presence of Lew Alcindor was the focal point of the action. That presence was not lost on the Knicks as they hurried shots, hesitated as if to see where he was before shooting, shot from outside their normal range, even refused to shoot when in range. In the first 12 minutes, the Knicks turned the ball over 10 times.

Once Alcindor scooped up a loose ball 10 feet from the basket, and flapping his arms like some giant bird spreading its wings, he wheeled around and jammed the ball into the basket with such fury that if Willis Reed had come a few inches closer, he, too, might have been stuffed into the basket.

The crowd gasped and the specter of Lew Alcindor was a frightening one. The capacity crowd of 19,500 shuddered at the thought of what this giant of a man could do to their beloved Knicks if he ever took charge. He did not take charge until it was too late.

In the second period, the game began to change. Reed used experience and girth to muscle Alcindor away from the boards, leaving the veteran Dave DeBusschere free to crash through for vital rebounds. The Knicks began passing more crisply and moving more rapidly to minimize the threat of Alcindor on defense.

Slowly, the Knicks began to draw away, their fast break often leaving Alcindor in arrears and the Knicks were able to get off shots before the big man could position himself to rebound or block. They hit the open man. They shot without hesitation and hit with almost unerring consistency. First DeBusschere, then Walt Frazier, then Dick Barnett, then Bill Bradley and, finally, Cazzie Russell.

You could see Alcindor slowly give way to rookie frustration as the points mounted on the Knicks' side and the mistakes mounted on the Milwaukee side.

Lew Alcindor was having trouble catching the ball. He fumbled Freddie Crawford's pass out of bounds and Reed came down on the other end and scored. He failed to handle a pass from Bob Dandridge and Reed came down on the other end and scored. He took a rebound and tossed a pass halfway downcourt .. into the arms of the Knicks' Walt Frazier. He came down with another rebound and had it taken away when three Knicks swiped at him like Lilliputians attacking Gulliver.

"Hey, Lew, you're a bum," came the taunts from behind the Knicks' bench. "You're a stiff."

They taunted him because they knew Lew

Alcindor is neither a bum nor a stiff. They taunted him because they were scared of him, really scared. He played with a controlled stoicism, his face a mask of non-expression. Only once did he give way to emotion, clenching his fists at his side in a self-rebuke for having lost the ball.

Several times he did not come down on offense, giving the impression of lack of interest or laziness and bringing more taunts from the fans. But it was not a lack of interest or laziness, it was the brief rest period he allows himself because he would play 47 minutes of the 48-minute game that night.

Larry Costello, his coach, had said that Lew gets lackadaisacal at times. With 58 seconds left in the game, after he had played 47 minutes and two seconds without rest, Alcindor was removed. When he came out, the Bucks trailed by 10, after being down by 19 points at one time. In the fourth period, Alcindor showed what it's like when he is on his game. In four and a half minutes, he scored 13 of Milwaukee's 17 points and cut eight points off the Knicks' lead.

When he left, he had scored 18 points in the fourth period and there were boos. Not boos of criticism, but boos of relief because Lew Alcindor had shown the Garden fans what he is capable of. He had shown them that their Knicks had better win their championship right away because the way Lew was coming on, next year would be too late.

The Knicks won the first game, 110-102, and statistically, the edge was Alcindor's over Reed. He scored 35 points to 24 for the Knick center, outrebounded him, 15-12, and had five assists to Reed's four. But most of the big Buck's damage had been done when it was too late. Reed had taken round one, but there were still six rounds to go.

"It can turn around," Lew said. "I don't know if it will, but it can. I just have to start making my shots. I don't think I played as well as I could have, but I'm not worried."

That was for the Knicks to do, worry about Alcindor, worry if he would put it all together in the next six games.

In Game No. 2, Alcindor did everything on a basketball court that a man can do.

"He would get the ball and wait for everybody to clear through so he had Willis one-on-one and then he'd go to work," said Walt Frazier. "And there was no way to stop him."

Alcindor scored 38 points, two more than Reed; he took 23 rebounds, four more than

Reed; he passed off for 11 assists, nine more than Reed. He made 16 of 25 from the field, but only six of 12 from the foul line and two of his misses came with 52 seconds to play and his team trailing, 110-109. The Bucks never caught up, losing the second game, 112-111, as the Knicks played at their most magnificent best.

Now the Bucks were going back home to familiar territory, back to Milwaukee knowing they had to get going or forget about a championship for this year.

The challenge in Game No. 3 was enormous and Alcindor responded. It was a game the Bucks could not afford to lose and so they went to their big guy.

It was the day after his 23rd birthday and Lew spent the afternoon of the big game in his apartment listening to records, the hip sounds of jazzmen Freddy Hubbard and Red Clay.

"It helps me get in harmony with the universe," he explained.

After the second game in New York when he had missed two crucial foul shots in the final minutes, he had showered, dressed and disappeared in record time. He refused to be drawn into lengthy discussion, answering the questions of the press with curt, monosyllabic replies.

The night of April 17 was different. It was the night in which Lew Alcindor finally put it all together, the night the Knicks had been fearing, but knew, in their hearts, would come sooner or later.

Milwaukee won the game 101-96, its first victory in the playoffs against New York. The Bucks won and made the series two games to one for the Knicks. Lew Alcindor scored 33 points, but the statistics sheet told only part of the story. It was his lowest point total, but his best game of the series.

The game is not played on the statistics sheet, it's played on the basketball court, and on the basketball court Lew was king. He grabbed 31 rebounds, 11 less than the entire Knick team, a personal high and a club record. The old record, 27, was Lew's too, made in his first game as a pro.

Still, the measure of the man was the manner in which he controlled the game of offense, intimidated the Knicks on defense and practically eliminated Reed (21 points, 10 rebounds) as a factor. He did all the things the Knicks knew, and feared, he might do one night.

"It was," said Milwaukee coach, Larry Costello, "a superb performance from Lew. It was the best game he's ever played as a pro. That's

194

my opinion. His might be different. I don't even know how many points he had, I still say this was his best game."

The thing about Alcindor was his presence . . . or omnipresence. He was everywhere, all over the court, blocking shots, stealing passes and frustrating the Knicks on defense and playing his typical, superlative game on offense.

Costello had made one change in the starting lineup, inserting the veteran Freddie Crawford in place of the slumping Flynn Robinson. The move was designed to give the Bucks more movement on offense, which was designed to get the ball more often to Alcindor. It worked.

And Alcindor helped make it work, mixing up his plays like Whitey Ford pitching at his best. When the ball came into him, Lew would hold it high above his head, then slip it to Bucks cutting off the low post. Or he would pitch it out and wait for the pattern to start all over again, until he could feed for an easy layup. He picked up five assists in this manner.

Often, too often for the Knicks, he would not pass. Instead, he would go irrepressibly toward the basket to toss in a short hook or to stuff one. And he was on the boards consistently tapping, rebounding or driving a missed shot home with his awesome stuff shot.

When he was removed from the game 14 seconds from the end and the Bucks comfortably in front, Alcindor threw his right arm toward the heavens in a gesture that was partly defiance, mostly victorious. He was acknowledging the standing ovation of the partisan crowd of 10,746 and a slight smile appeared on his face, that face that is always expressionless on the court, as he accepted the congratulations of his teammates in the skin-to-skin, slap-slap that has become the athletes' handshake.

He smiled because he knew he had done the big job, had proved something to his teammates, to the Knicks, to the fans, to himself. It was his first game as a 23-year-old and it was as if he had found instant maturity on the court; as if he had pushed that other Lew Alcindor, that young, immature, 22-year-old Lew Alcindor out of existence.

He had struck, finally, and the Knicks knew they would have to prevent him from doing the same thing three more times in the next four games.

It is impossible to figure the game of basketball, impossible to understand why a man can be the dominant force one night and practically not a factor at all two days later. What makes it even more impossible to understand is that the Bucks, who won with Alcindor scoring 33 points, could not win with Lew getting 38.

Again, it is because points alone do not count. Where Alcindor had grabbed a record 31 rebounds in Game No. 3, he took only nine in the fourth game. Where he had made five assists in the third game, he made only one in the fourth. Where he was all over the court, blocking shots and intimidating the Knicks in the third game, they were practically unaware of his presence in the fourth game.

The Knicks had sprinted to a 20-point lead at half-time, watched it practically vanish under a furious Milwaukee comeback in the third period, then stormed back in the fourth as Cazzie Russell came off the bench to score 18 points and lead the 117-105 New York victory.

Now the teams were going back to New York, back where the Knicks could wrap up the series and put down the Milwaukee menace for the year.

In New York, the Bucks were no match for the streaking Knicks, who could sense the kill. Playing their most complete and their most effective game, they spurted to a 35-19 lead at the quarter, increased it to 69-45 at the half and to 101-72 after three quarters.

There was no stopping the New Yorkers this

night, although Alcindor did his best. He scored 27 points and pulled down 11 rebounds, but with 2:11 remaining in the third period and the Bucks trailing by 40, Costello removed his star and Lew sat on the bench for the rest of the game.

"It would have been redundant to put me back in," Lew said later.

He sat there, in the middle of huge Madison Square Garden and the 19,500 fans were having a gay time and some of them sang a lullaby to Lew.

"Goodbye Lewie," they sang to the tune of "Goodnight Ladies":

"Goodbye Lewie, Goodbye Lewie, Goodbye Lewie,
"We hate to see you go."

They sang, Alcindor supposed, "because they're scared. I've always had that happen to me whenever I've played in New York. I can't feel badly about it, it's their problem. If they want to act that way, that's their business.

"We've got nothing to be ashamed of. We're a very young team and we probably shouldn't have been here in the first place, playing for the eastern division championship."

The Knicks, too, were perplexed and embarrassed by the impromptu, sarcastic uncalled-for serenade.

"I don't think he deserved it," said Dave De-Busschere. "He gave his all in this series."

"I don't think they meant it in a derogatory sense," guessed Willis Reed. "Garden fans are not that way. Lew's just a rookie, remember, and he showed great poise."

"It was more of a sigh of relief than anything else," Walt Frazier insisted. "They were glad he lost, glad to get rid of him because they know he's a helluva ball player."

When it was over, Alcindor and Guy Rodgers led a procession of Bucks across the long corridor into the jammed and joyous Knick dressing room. They went to each member of the Knicks to shake hands and wish them luck and then Lew Alcindor went to the center of the room where Willis Reed was surrounded by more than a dozen reporters. He reached over and extended his long arm over the reporters and Reed took Alcindor's extended hand.

"Good going," Lew Alcindor said, "take the whole thing."

Then he turned and walked out of the room and across the hall to his own dressing room. It was quiet in the Milwaukee dressing room.

There was disappointment there, but there was not dejection. The young Bucks knew their time had not yet come.

Lew Alcindor dressed slowly and went outside to join his father, who was waiting for him there in the corridor.

Lew Alcindor's first year as a professional had come to an end. But, in truth, it was not the end, it was only the beginning.

14
Epilogue

The strains of "Goodbye Lewie" as sung by the Madison Square Garden chorale had barely died down when the Milwaukee Bucks completed a deal that would make them change their tune. It brought the fabulous, all-time great Oscar Robertson to the Bucks.

The thought of the Big O and the Big A combining their enormous talents was a prospect that excited people in Milwaukee and frightened people everywhere else. And there was the promise of great things for the future as the young Milwaukee center looked back on his first professional season with the mixed emotions of despair and determination to do better.

"I'd like to think I've improved in every way," he said. "I'm getting used to what's going on out there."

In New York, Ned Irish, president of the Knicks, had made a prophetic remark during the New York-Milwaukee playoff of Abdul-Jabbar's rookie season.

"I hope we beat them," the Knick president said. "I think it's the last realistic chance anybody will have for a while."

A year later, Irish's words came true. Alcindor, now known by his Islamic name of Kareem Abdul-Jabbar, was the driving force in leading the Milwaukee Bucks to their first NBA championship. It was only the third year of the team's existence.

Abdul-Jabbar played spectacularly, and with Robertson providing a steadying, veteran influence, the Bucks reached the pinnacle of professional basketball in the 1970-71 season. They were, perhaps, years ahead of their time, but they were a team that would not be stopped.

They had won a remarkable 80 percent of their games during the regular season, losing only 16 out of 82. And they kept right on rolling in the playoffs. The San Francisco Warriors were eliminated in five games; the Los Angeles Lakers were beaten in five games; and then the championship was theirs when the Baltimore Bullets were swept in four games. It was the first four-game series in the history of the NBA's playoff finals.

Abdul-Jabbar was devastating. He averaged 26.6 points and 17 rebounds for 14 playoff games and was clearly the outstanding player in the playoffs.

With Kareem Abdul-Jabbar as their leader, the Bucks had a dynasty in the making; a dynasty to rival the one enjoyed by the Boston Celtics through 1968. Bill Russell and Company won 11 NBA championships in 13 years. It was a record Kareem Abdul-Jabbar and Company could shoot for, a record not out of their reach.

Abdul-Jabbar would continue to improve. He would improve to the point where he would be like nobody before him, combining, as Bob Cousy once said, "the mental concentration of Bill Russell and the physical dominance of Wilt Chamberlain."

But basketball is not a one-man game; if it were, there would be no doubt which one man would reign as its champion. It is a five-man game. In the years ahead, Abdul-Jabbar could not do it alone.

Oscar Robertson grew older. Injuries, the little hurts with which an athlete must frequently play, came more often and lasted longer. A few trades did not produce their desired effect, and no rookie came along to fill in for aging and departed veterans.

In the 1971-72 season, Kareem Abdul-Jabbar won his second consecutive NBA scoring championship with an average of 34.8 and was voted the league's Most Valuable Player as the Bucks won an astonishing 77 percent of their regular season games to win in the Midwest Division with a record of 63-19.

But the Los Angeles Lakers were even more astonishing. They finished with a league record of 69 victories and 13 defeats, a winning percentage of .841. Included among those 69 victories were 33 in a row, another league record, which was stopped by Abdul-Jabbar and the Bucks in Milwaukee on January 7, 1972.

The Bucks beat San Francisco in their first round playoff series, four games to one, but this was to be the year of the Lakers. In the Western Conference finals, they eliminated the young Bucks in six games.

In the 1972-73 playoffs, the Bucks suffered one of those frequent let-downs that happen in sports and were eliminated in the first round in six games by the San Francisco Warriors, a team that had won 13 fewer games than Milwaukee in the regular season.

By 1973-74, the once-great Boston Celtics had returned to the top of basketball with a team that presented a new concept in basketball. Height and strength were replaced by speed and aggressiveness and once again, in the playoff finals, five-man basketball triumphed over one-man basketball.

Abdul-Jabbar was sensational, but he couldn't do it alone. He scored 35 points in the first game, and the Bucks lost, 98-83. He led them to victory in Game No. 2 with 36 points, but scored 26 points in the third game and the Bucks lost, 95-83.

It was that kind of see-saw struggle with Abdul-Jabbar taking on wave after wave of Celtics. His 37 points in the fifth game were wasted, as the rest of the Bucks scored only 50. And with a chance to win the championship, Abdul-Jabbar's desperation hook shot missed at the buzzer and the Celtics won the sixth game in overtime.

With that lease on life, the Celtics ran over the Bucks in the seventh game for the championship. Kareem Abdul-Jabbar was the highest scorer in the series. It was no consolation to Kareem, who contemplated what lay ahead.

"What I want to do," Abdul-Jabbar says, "is play 10 or 12 years in the NBA and see what I can do against the big guys. Then I'll go back to more normal things."

It has always been important to Kareem that he succeed in pro basketball. It is important to his pride, to his self-satisfaction. But he is not a man who will waste what he has been able to achieve on the basketball court.

The future?

"I don't know," he says. "I always liked teaching. Maybe I'll teach. Maybe I'll do social work. Whatever I do, I'm pretty sure it will be with black kids. That's not because I'm preju-diced against white kids. But I was a black kid. I know their scene. I know how to talk to them. I mean something to them.

"People think I'm even taller than I am. They think I'm maybe seven-three or seven-four," he once said. "That's because I stand tall. My father taught me that as a child. I have always stood tall. I have always been proud of my height and proud of myself. That's where I think I can help other black kids. I want them all to stand tall."

Wherever he goes, whatever he does, whom-ever he does it for, you can be sure Kareem

Abdul-Jabbar will be successful. He works too hard at being successful to fail. And he will work just as hard after he is finished with basketball as he has worked to succeed in basketball.

That is Kareem Abdul-Jabbar's style.

About the Author

Phil Pepe has been a Kareem Abdul-Jabbar-watcher since 1961, when the author first met him and wrote the first newspaper story ever written about him. Abdul-Jabbar was Lew Alcindor then, a 13-year-old eighth grader who stood 6 feet, 8 inches tall.

Pepe has written five pieces for national magazines (*Pageant*, *Sport*, *Basketball Yearbook*) as well as dozens of newspaper articles with Abdul-Jabbar as the subject.

His newspaper experience includes eleven years with the New York *World Telegram & Sun*, later the *World Journal Tribune*. He joined the staff of the New York *Daily News* in 1968. His newspaper assignments have taken him all over the U.S., covering every World Series since 1960 (except 1967), the Kentucky Derby, United States Open Golf Championship, the first Super Bowl, and NBA playoffs. He has covered more than a dozen world's heavyweight championship fights on three continents, including the 1974 Ali-Foreman fight in Zaire (Africa).

His eleven books include *Winners Never Quit*, *No-Hitter*, *From Ghetto To Glory: The Story of Bob Gibson*, Gibson's autobiography, *A View from the Rim*, *Willis Reed on Basketball*, *Greatest Stars of the NBA*, and *The Wit and Wisdom of Yogi Berra*.

He was born in 1935 in New York City. A graduate of St. John's University, he and his wife and four children live in Upper Saddle River, N. J.

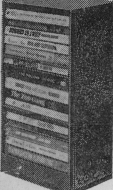